AMAZING SPIDER-MAN: FAMILY BUSINESS

First printing 2018.
ISBN 978-0-7851-8441-6.

Published by MARVEL WORLDWIDE, INC., a
subsidiary of MARVEL ENTERTAINMENT, LLC.
OFFICE OF PUBLICATION: 135 West 50th
Street, New York, NY 10020. Copyright ©
2018 MARVEL. No similarity between any of
the names, characters, persons, and/or
institutions in this magazine with those of
any living or dead person or institution is
intended, and any such similarity which may
exist is purely coincidental.

Printed in the U.S.A.

For information regarding advertising in
Marvel Comics or on Marvel.com, please
contact Vit DeBellis, Custom Solutions &
Integrated Advertising Manager, at
vdebellis@marvel.com. For Marvel
subscription inquiries, please call
888-511-5480.

**Manufactured between 5/4/2018 and
6/5/2018 by LSC COMMUNICATIONS INC.,
KENDALLVILLE, IN, USA.**

10 9 8 7 6 5 4 3 2 1

MARK WAID and JAMES ROBINSON
Writers

GABRIELE DELL'OTTO
Painted Art

WERTHER DELL'EDERA
Pencils

VC's Joe Caramagna
Letters

Ellie Pyle and Tom Brennan
Associate Editors

Stephen Wacker
Editor

Jennifer Grünwald
Collection Editor

Caitlin O'Connell
Assistant Editor

Kateri Woody
Associate Managing Editor

Mark D. Beazley
Editor, Special Projects

Jeff Youngquist
VP Production & Special Projects

David Gabriel
SVP Print, Sales & Marketing

Rian Hughes
Book Designer

C.B. Cebulski
Editor In Chief

Joe Quesada
Chief Creative Officer

Dan Buckley
President

Alan Fine
Executive Producer

Special thanks to
Christopher Yost

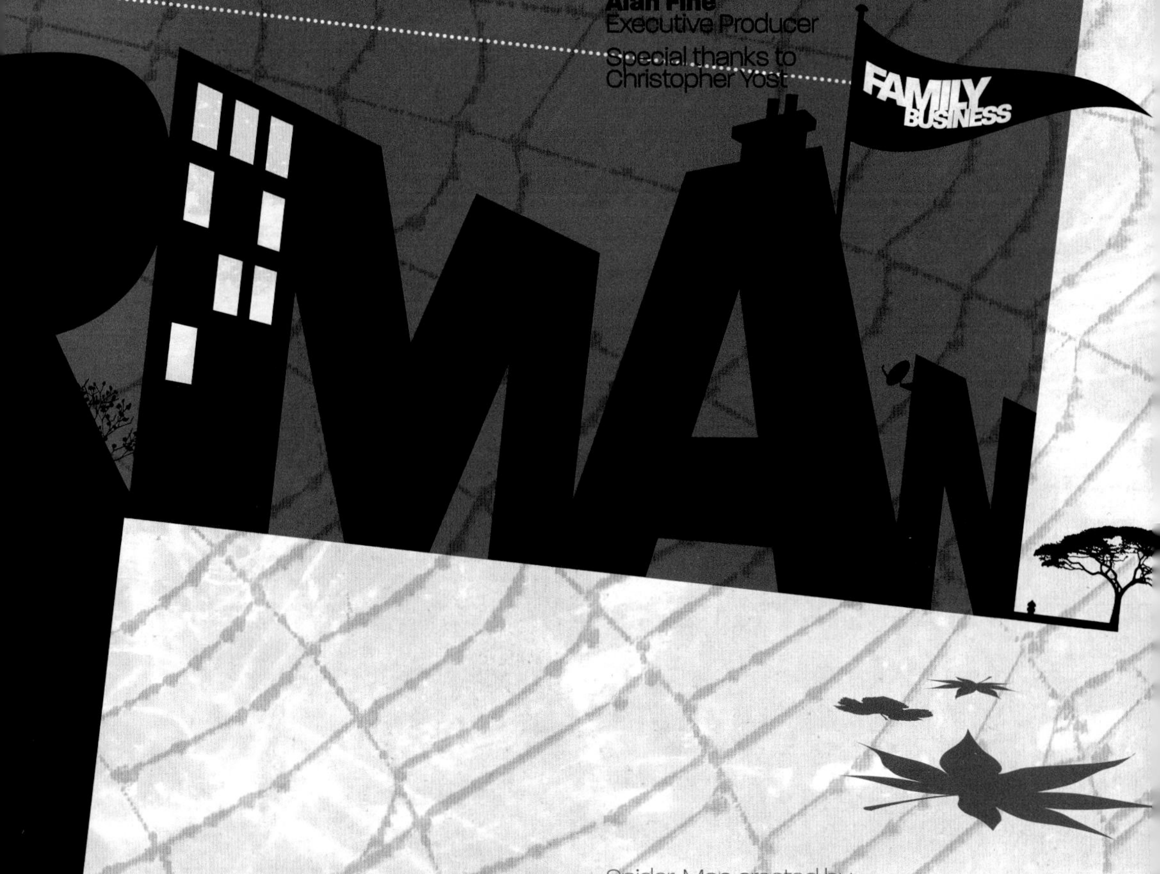
FAMILY
BUSINESS

Spider-Man created by
Stan Lee & Steve Ditko

Tell me a **Spider-Man** story.
And make it a good one.

We all know **Spidey.**

He's been part of our culture for more than half a century. He's in comic books, movies and cartoons. Action figures, lunchboxes and pajamas. And we all know his story...

Peter Parker—bitten by a radioactive spider—gains Great Power but learns it comes with a price: Great Responsibility.

That lesson is at the character's core and has been the fuel for every great **Spidey** story for 50 years.

So how do you keep that up and keep it fresh? How can you find a new responsibility for Pete? What will have us anxiously flipping to the next page? What's that twist no **Spidey** scribe's thought of before?

And that's where **Mark Waid** and **James Robinson** deliver. They drive this story right up to you in a super-charged sports car, fling open the door and yell, "Jump in"—and you're off! They're taking you and **Spidey** to places he's never been... with a mysterious new character who changes everything.

Family Business gives you all the Spidey action, twists, and turns you could want—all gorgeously brought to life by **Gabriele Dell'Otto** and **Werther Dell'Edera.** This is more than a comic you'll read—it's one you'll reread. Not just a good **Spidey** story, but a ***great*** one!

Dan Slott
December 2013

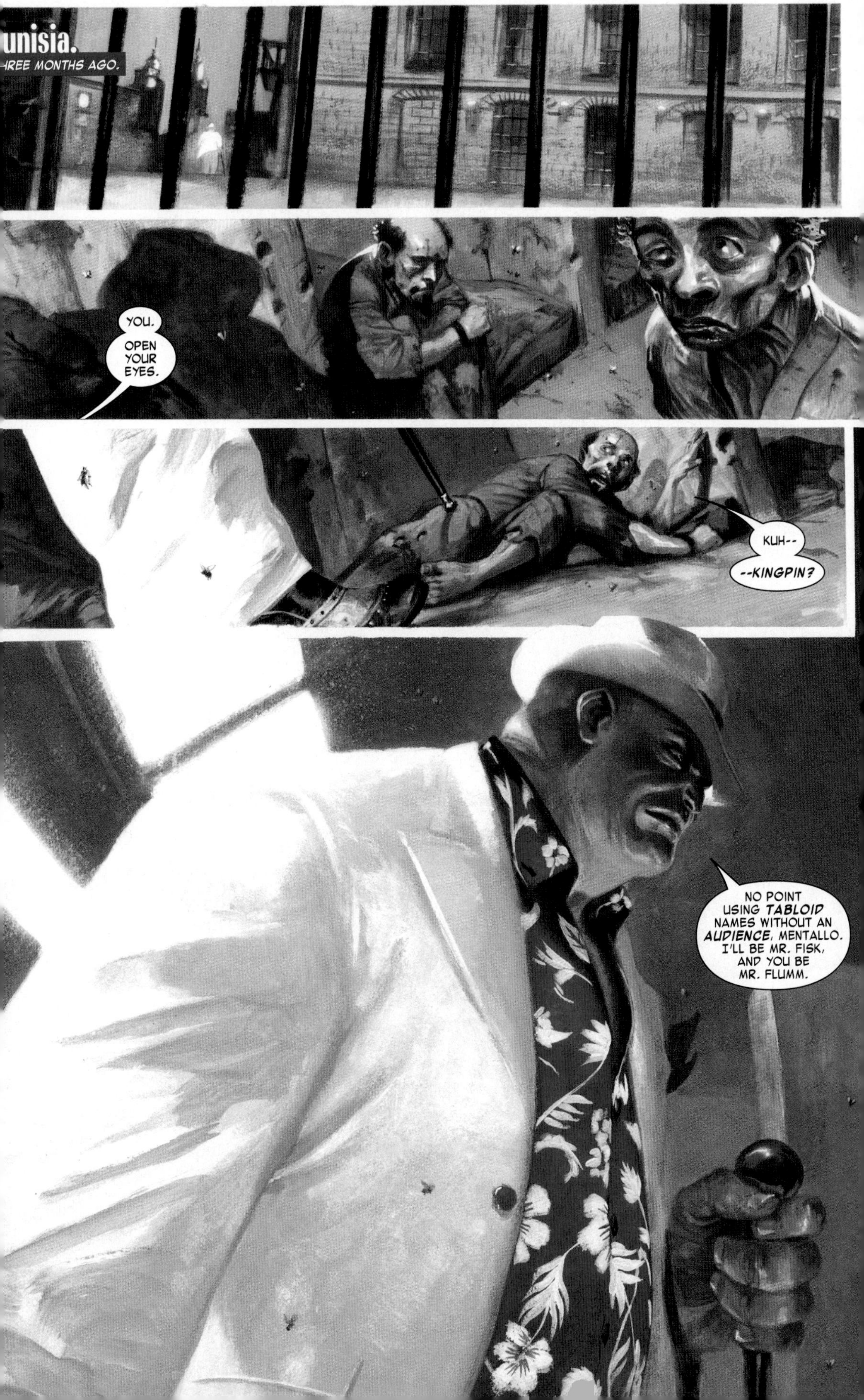

unisia.
HREE MONTHS AGO.
YOU.
OPEN YOUR EYES.
KUH--
--KINGPIN?
NO POINT USING TABLOID NAMES WITHOUT AN AUDIENCE, MENTALLO. I'LL BE MR. FISK, AND YOU BE MR. FLUMM.

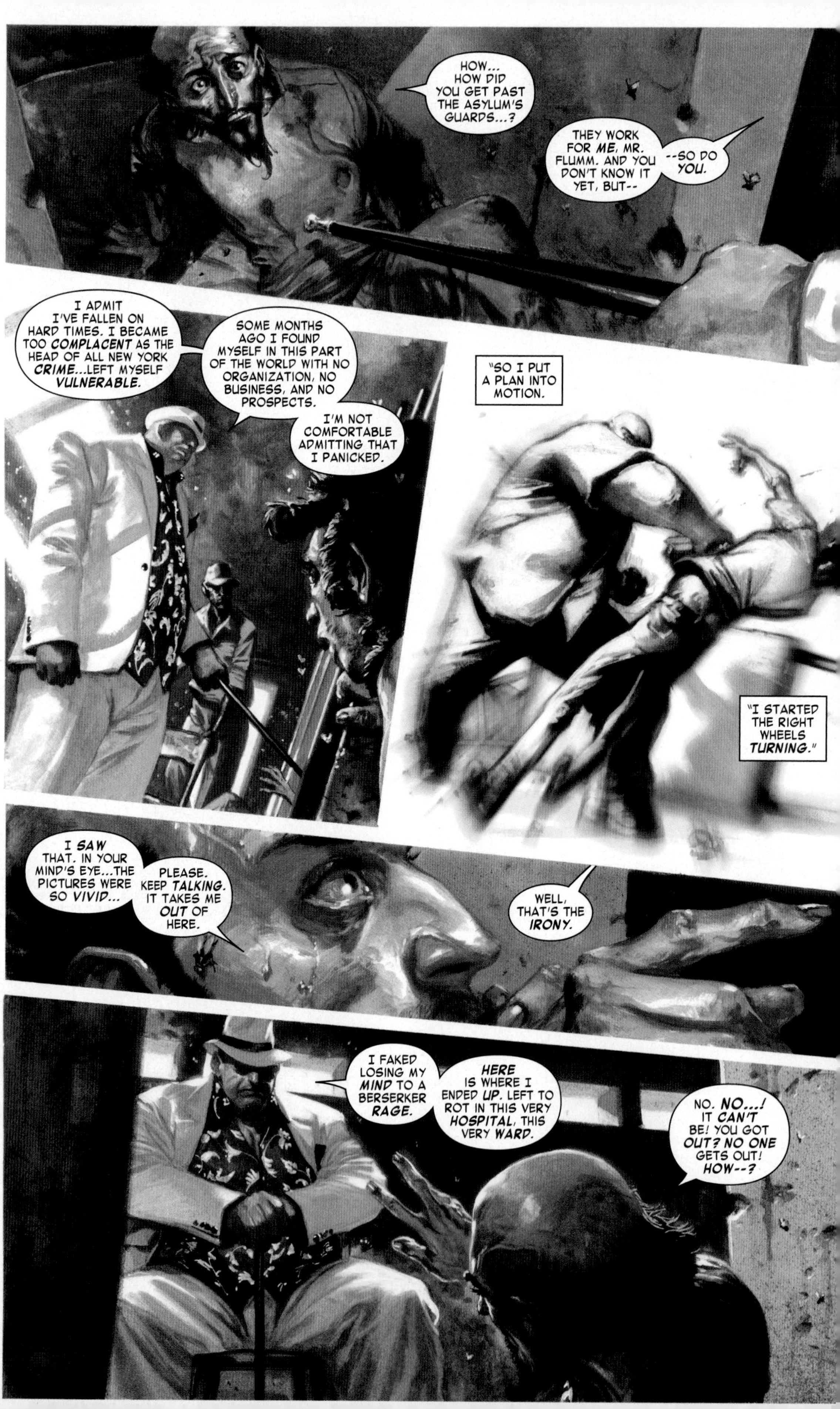
HOW... HOW DID YOU GET PAST THE ASYLUM'S GUARDS...?
THEY WORK FOR ME, MR. FLUMM. AND YOU DON'T KNOW IT YET, BUT--
--SO DO YOU.
I ADMIT I'VE FALLEN ON HARD TIMES. I BECAME TOO COMPLACENT AS THE HEAD OF ALL NEW YORK CRIME...LEFT MYSELF VULNERABLE.
SOME MONTHS AGO I FOUND MYSELF IN THIS PART OF THE WORLD WITH NO ORGANIZATION, NO BUSINESS, AND NO PROSPECTS.
I'M NOT COMFORTABLE ADMITTING THAT I PANICKED.
"SO I PUT A PLAN INTO MOTION.
"I STARTED THE RIGHT WHEELS TURNING."
I SAW THAT. IN YOUR MIND'S EYE...THE PICTURES WERE SO VIVID...
PLEASE. KEEP TALKING. IT TAKES ME OUT OF HERE.
WELL, THAT'S THE IRONY.
I FAKED LOSING MY MIND TO A BERSERKER RAGE.
HERE IS WHERE I ENDED UP. LEFT TO ROT IN THIS VERY HOSPITAL, THIS VERY WARD.
NO. NO...! IT CAN'T BE! YOU GOT OUT? NO ONE GETS OUT! HOW--?

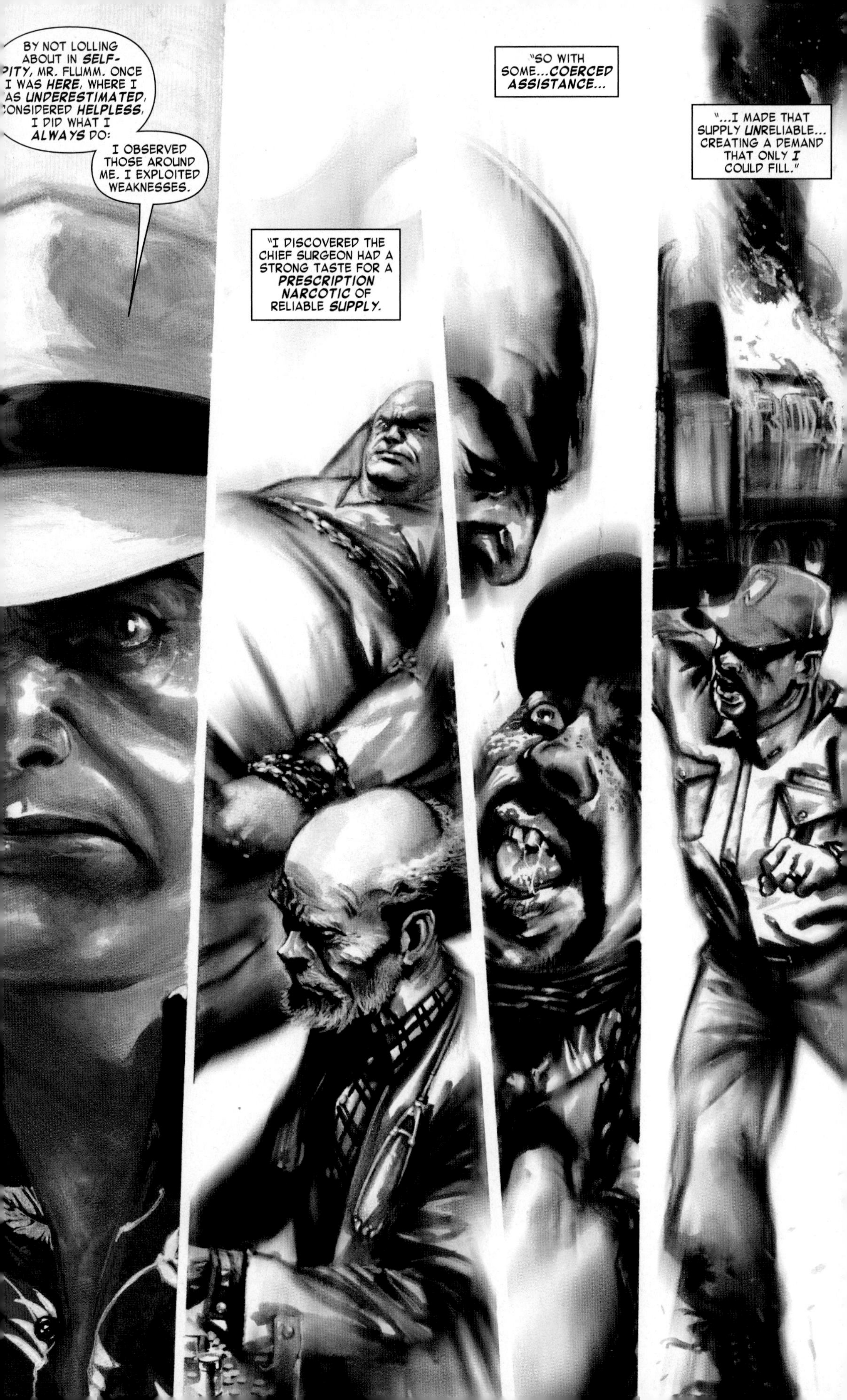
BY NOT LOLLING ABOUT IN SELF-PITY, MR. FLUMM. ONCE I WAS HERE, WHERE I WAS UNDERESTIMATED, CONSIDERED HELPLESS, I DID WHAT I ALWAYS DO:
I OBSERVED THOSE AROUND ME. I EXPLOITED WEAKNESSES.
"I DISCOVERED THE CHIEF SURGEON HAD A STRONG TASTE FOR A PRESCRIPTION NARCOTIC OF RELIABLE SUPPLY.
"SO WITH SOME...COERCED ASSISTANCE...
"...I MADE THAT SUPPLY UNRELIABLE... CREATING A DEMAND THAT ONLY I COULD FILL."

BEFORE LONG, THE CHIEF SURGEON WAS ONLY TOO GLAD TO *RELEASE* ME...AND TO GRANT ME *ANOTHER* FAVOR:

WAREHOUSING *YOU* IN AN ATMOSPHERE THAT WOULD *NULLIFY* YOUR TELEPATHIC POWERS UNTIL I COULD PUT THEM TO *USE*.

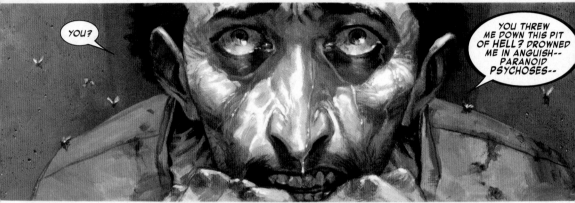

YOU?

YOU THREW ME DOWN THIS PIT OF *HELL?* DROWNED ME IN ANGUISH-- PARANOID *PSYCHOSES--*

I FEEL THEIR SUFFERING *PLUS* MY *OWN!* LIKE HOT COALS ON MY *BRAIN!* YOU PUT ME *HERE?* YOU *PLANNED* THIS?

TUT, TUT. THAT'S ALL IN THE *PAST,* MR. FLUMM.

I BROUGHT YOU A *GIFT.*

YOU DON'T LIKE THE WRETCH YOU'VE *BECOME?*

HOW WOULD YOU LIKE TO BE *SOMEONE ELSE...?*

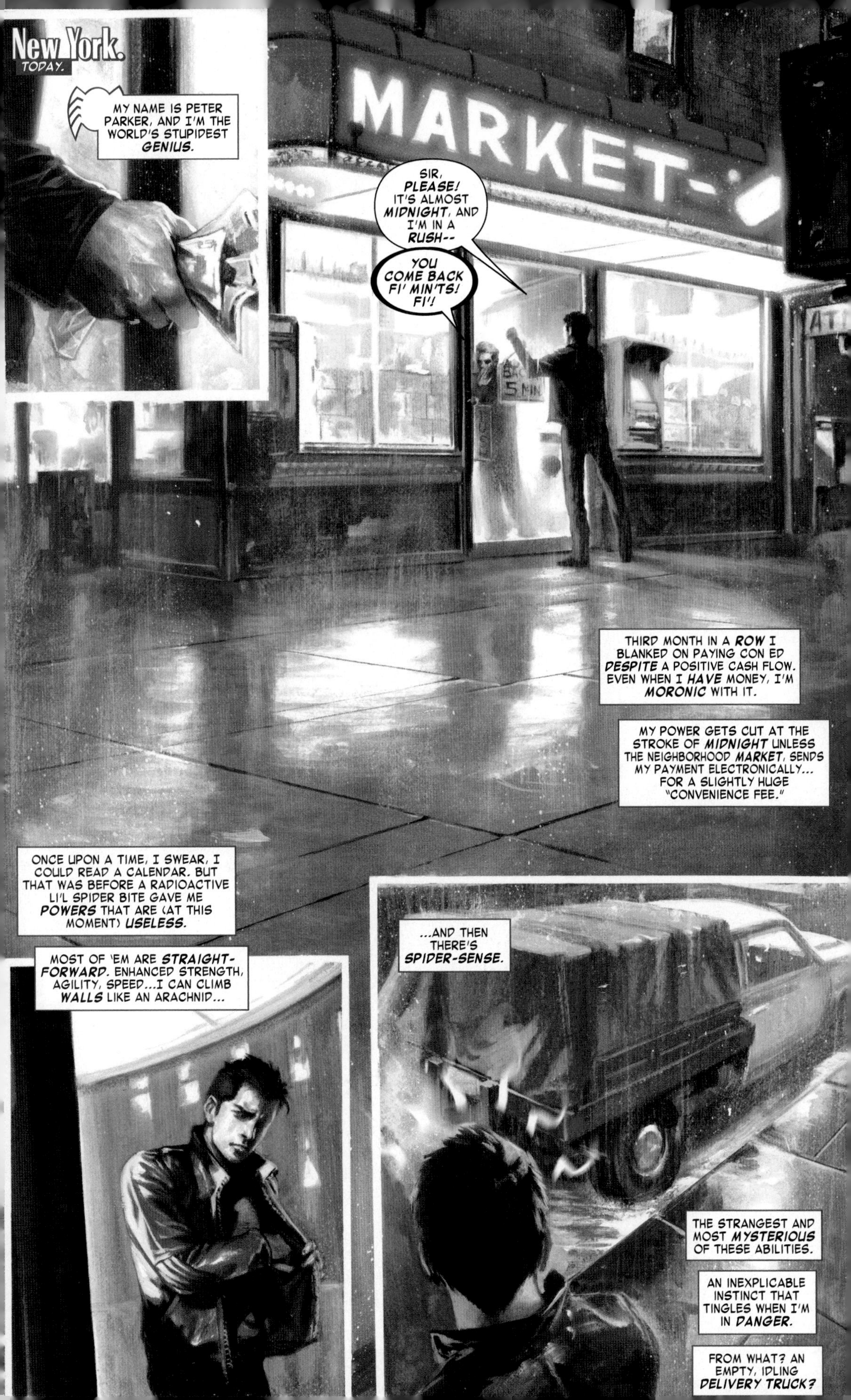
New York.
TODAY.
MY NAME IS PETER PARKER, AND I'M THE WORLD'S STUPIDEST GENIUS.
SIR, PLEASE! IT'S ALMOST MIDNIGHT, AND I'M IN A RUSH--
YOU COME BACK FI' MIN'TS! FI'!
MARKET
THIRD MONTH IN A ROW I BLANKED ON PAYING CON ED DESPITE A POSITIVE CASH FLOW. EVEN WHEN I HAVE MONEY, I'M MORONIC WITH IT.
MY POWER GETS CUT AT THE STROKE OF MIDNIGHT UNLESS THE NEIGHBORHOOD MARKET, SENDS MY PAYMENT ELECTRONICALLY... FOR A SLIGHTLY HUGE "CONVENIENCE FEE."
ONCE UPON A TIME, I SWEAR, I COULD READ A CALENDAR. BUT THAT WAS BEFORE A RADIOACTIVE LI'L SPIDER BITE GAVE ME POWERS THAT ARE (AT THIS MOMENT) USELESS.
MOST OF 'EM ARE STRAIGHT-FORWARD. ENHANCED STRENGTH, AGILITY, SPEED...I CAN CLIMB WALLS LIKE AN ARACHNID...
...AND THEN THERE'S SPIDER-SENSE.
THE STRANGEST AND MOST MYSTERIOUS OF THESE ABILITIES.
AN INEXPLICABLE INSTINCT THAT TINGLES WHEN I'M IN DANGER.
FROM WHAT? AN EMPTY, IDLING DELIVERY TRUCK?

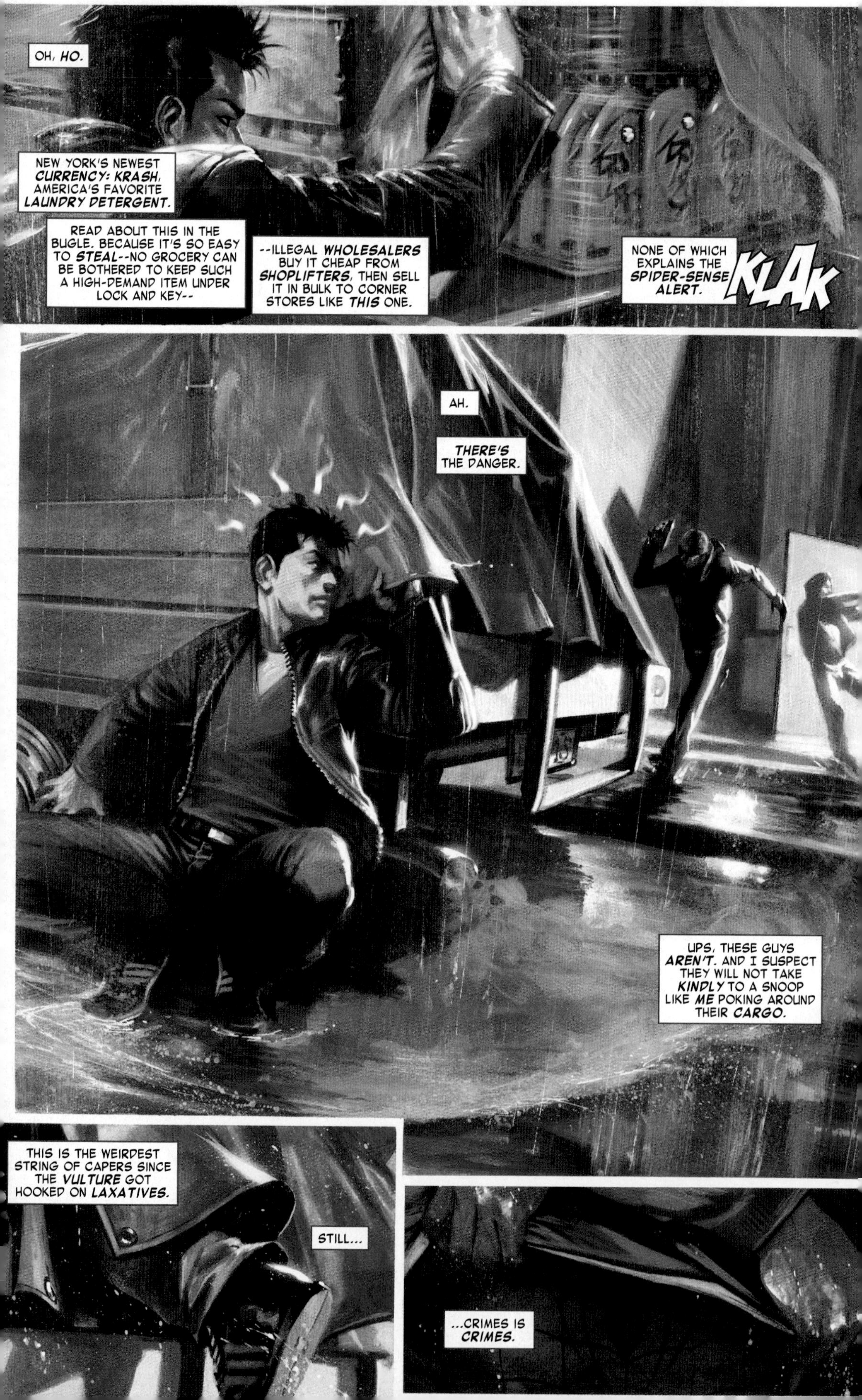
OH, HO.
NEW YORK'S NEWEST CURRENCY: KRASH, AMERICA'S FAVORITE LAUNDRY DETERGENT.
READ ABOUT THIS IN THE BUGLE. BECAUSE IT'S SO EASY TO STEAL--NO GROCERY CAN BE BOTHERED TO KEEP SUCH A HIGH-DEMAND ITEM UNDER LOCK AND KEY--
--ILLEGAL WHOLESALERS BUY IT CHEAP FROM SHOPLIFTERS, THEN SELL IT IN BULK TO CORNER STORES LIKE THIS ONE.
NONE OF WHICH EXPLAINS THE SPIDER-SENSE ALERT.
KLAK
AH.
THERE'S THE DANGER.
UPS, THESE GUYS AREN'T. AND I SUSPECT THEY WILL NOT TAKE KINDLY TO A SNOOP LIKE ME POKING AROUND THEIR CARGO.
THIS IS THE WEIRDEST STRING OF CAPERS SINCE THE VULTURE GOT HOOKED ON LAXATIVES.
STILL...
...CRIMES IS CRIMES.

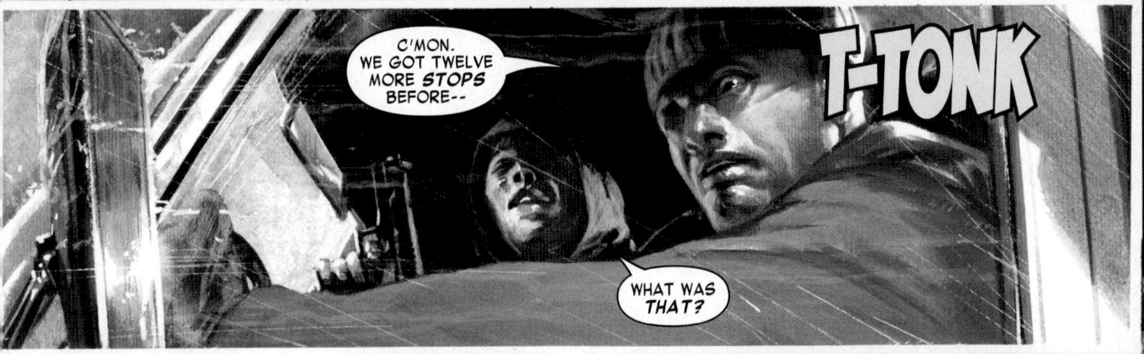
C'MON. WE GOT TWELVE MORE STOPS BEFORE--
T-TONK
WHAT WAS THAT?

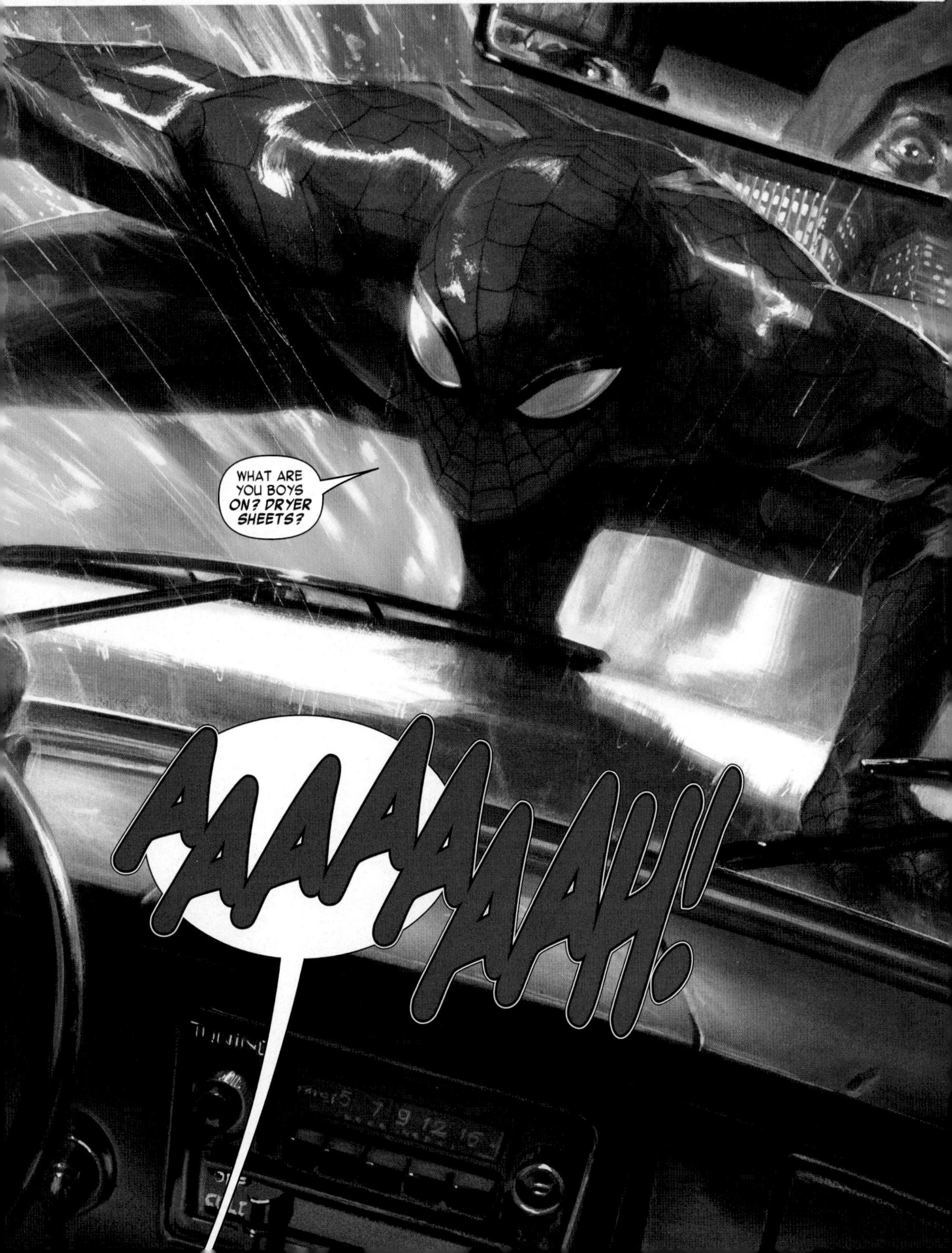
WHAT ARE YOU BOYS ON? DRYER SHEETS?
AAAAAAAAH!

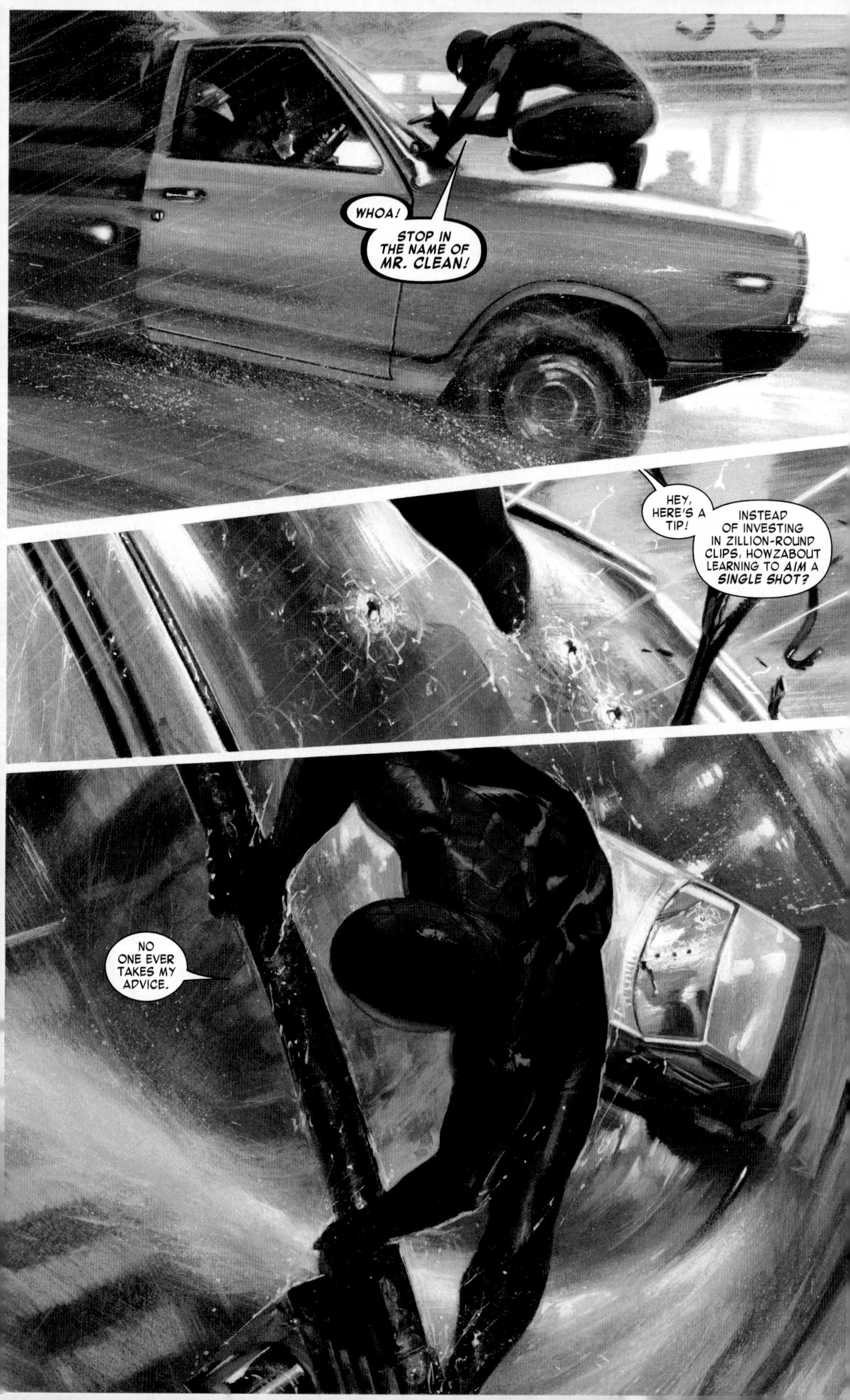
WHOA!
STOP IN THE NAME OF MR. CLEAN!
HEY, HERE'S A TIP!
INSTEAD OF INVESTING IN ZILLION-ROUND CLIPS, HOWZABOUT LEARNING TO AIM A SINGLE SHOT?
NO ONE EVER TAKES MY ADVICE.

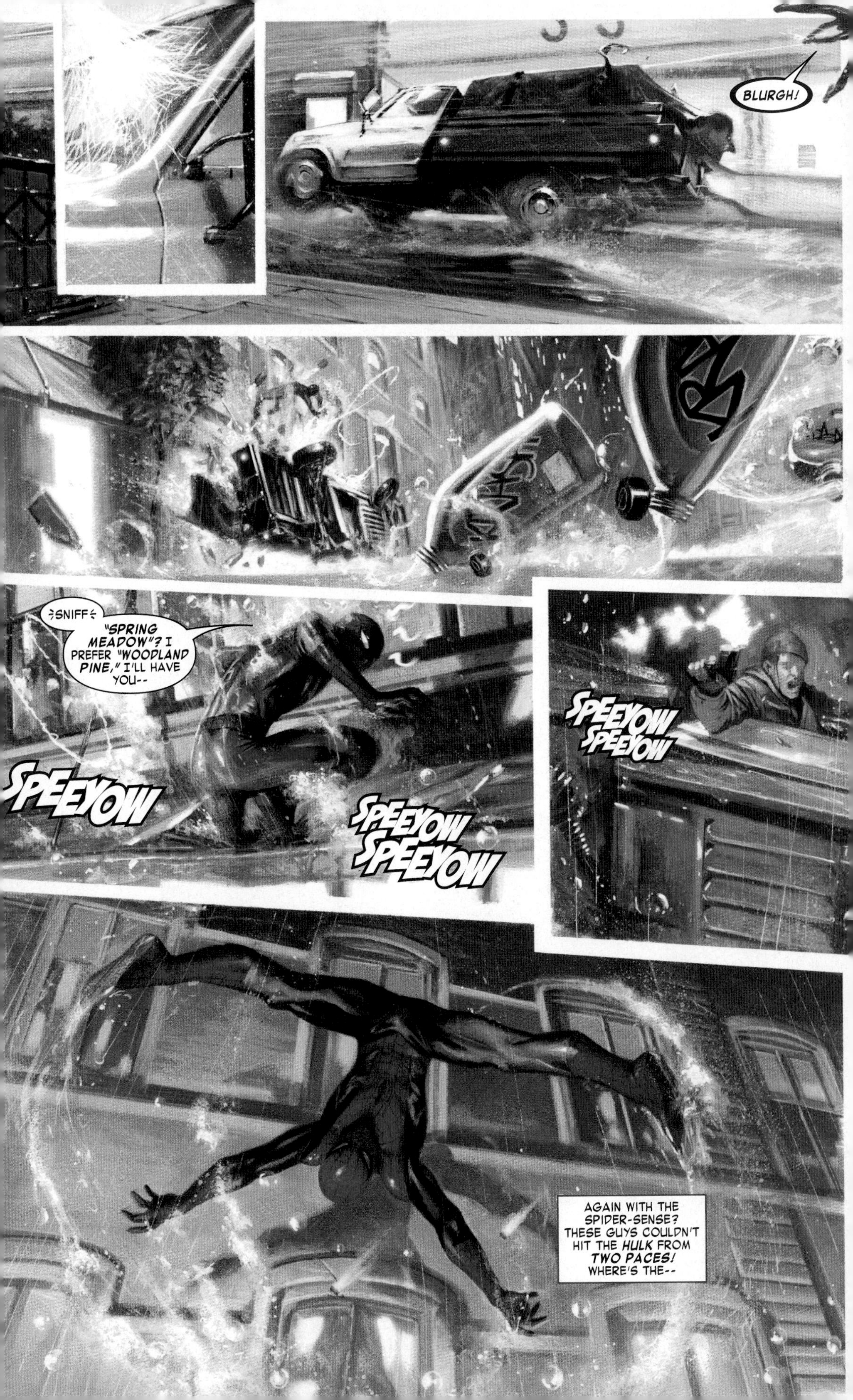

BLURGH!
⋟SNIFF⋞
"SPRING MEADOW"? I PREFER "WOODLAND PINE," I'LL HAVE YOU--
SPEEYOW
SPEEYOW SPEEYOW
SPEEYOW SPEEYOW
AGAIN WITH THE SPIDER-SENSE? THESE GUYS COULDN'T HIT THE HULK FROM TWO PACES! WHERE'S THE--

--DANGER--?
STUPID
SOAP.
THWIPPP
TRY SOAKING THIS OUT, JERKS!
THWIPPP
GOOD NEWS! LOOKS LIKE YOUR RIDE IS HERE!
NOW, WHERE ARE MY CLOTHES--?
UCH.

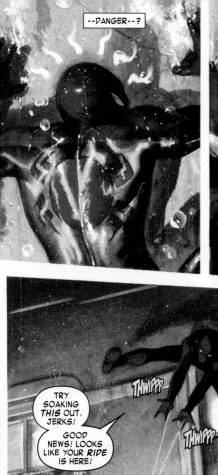

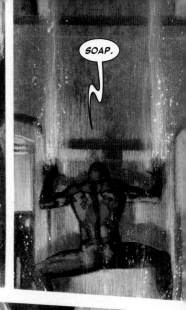

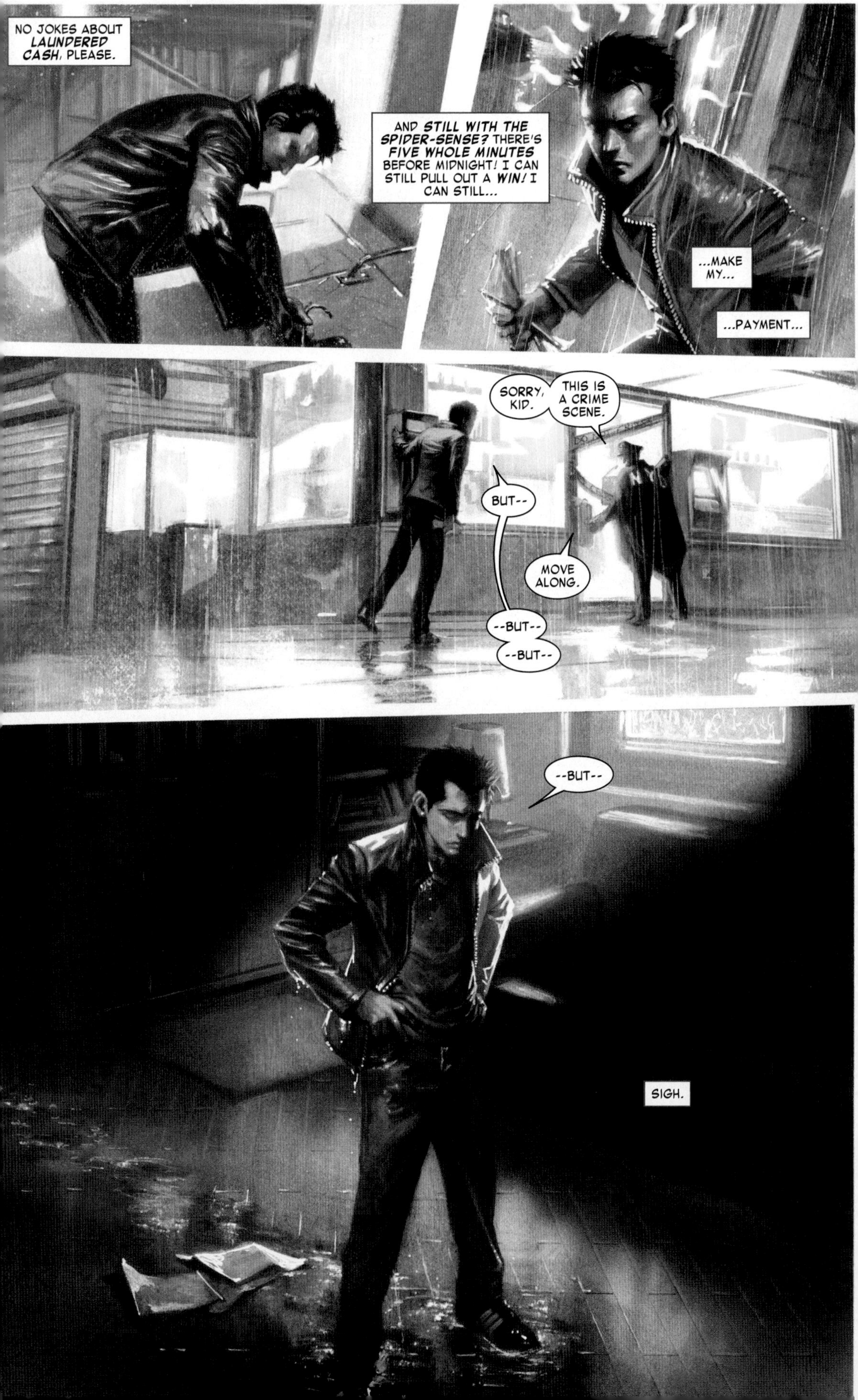
NO JOKES ABOUT LAUNDERED CASH, PLEASE.
AND STILL WITH THE SPIDER-SENSE? THERE'S FIVE WHOLE MINUTES BEFORE MIDNIGHT! I CAN STILL PULL OUT A WIN! I CAN STILL...
...MAKE MY...
...PAYMENT...
SORRY, KID.
THIS IS A CRIME SCENE.
BUT--
MOVE ALONG.
--BUT--
--BUT--
--BUT--
SIGH.

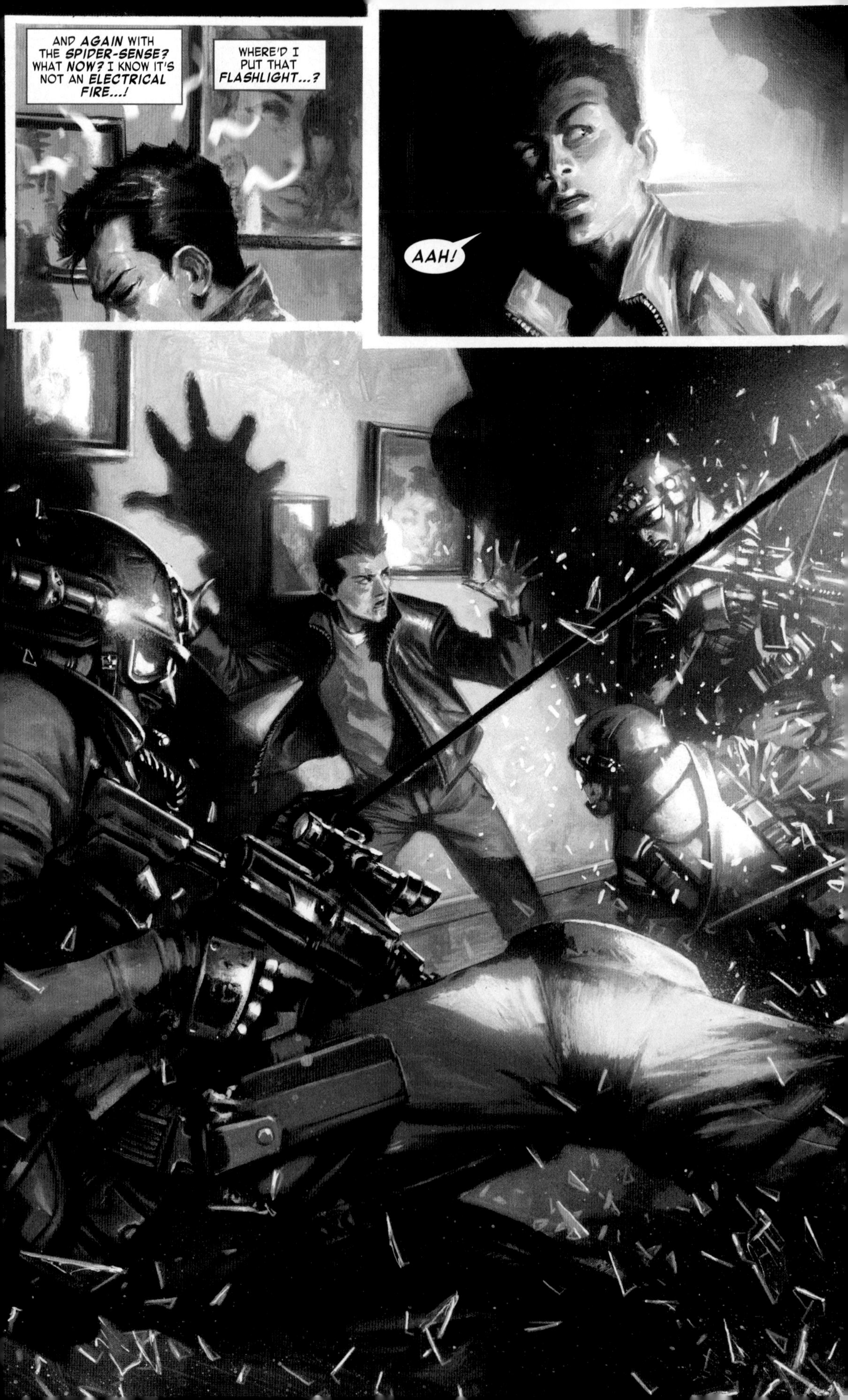
AND AGAIN WITH THE SPIDER-SENSE? WHAT NOW? I KNOW IT'S NOT AN ELECTRICAL FIRE...!
WHERE'D I PUT THAT FLASHLIGHT...?
AAH!

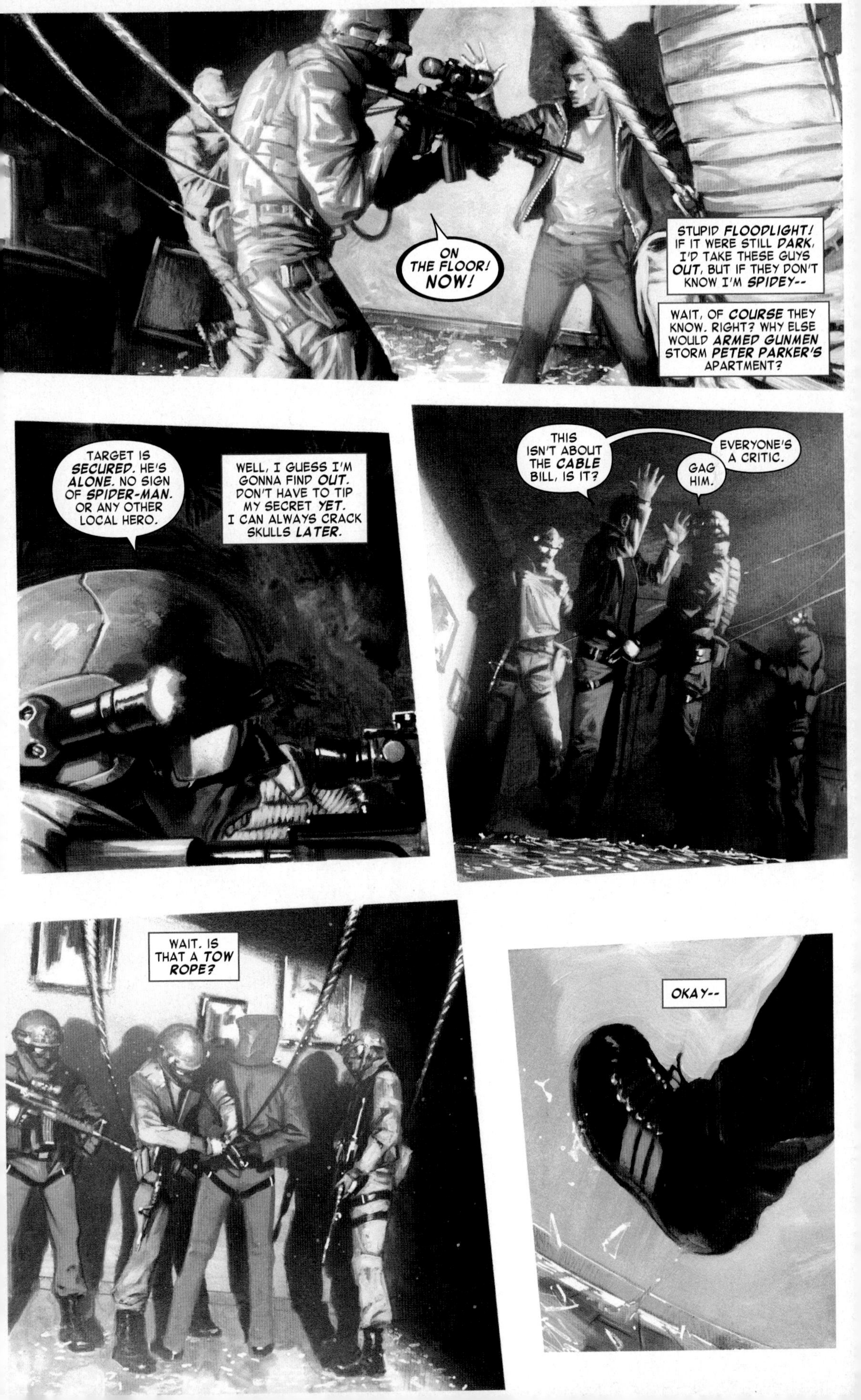
ON THE FLOOR! NOW!
STUPID FLOODLIGHT! IF IT WERE STILL DARK, I'D TAKE THESE GUYS OUT, BUT IF THEY DON'T KNOW I'M SPIDEY--
WAIT, OF COURSE THEY KNOW. RIGHT? WHY ELSE WOULD ARMED GUNMEN STORM PETER PARKER'S APARTMENT?
TARGET IS SECURED. HE'S ALONE. NO SIGN OF SPIDER-MAN. OR ANY OTHER LOCAL HERO.
WELL, I GUESS I'M GONNA FIND OUT. DON'T HAVE TO TIP MY SECRET YET. I CAN ALWAYS CRACK SKULLS LATER.
THIS ISN'T ABOUT THE CABLE BILL, IS IT?
EVERYONE'S A CRITIC.
GAG HIM.
WAIT. IS THAT A TOW ROPE?
OKAY--

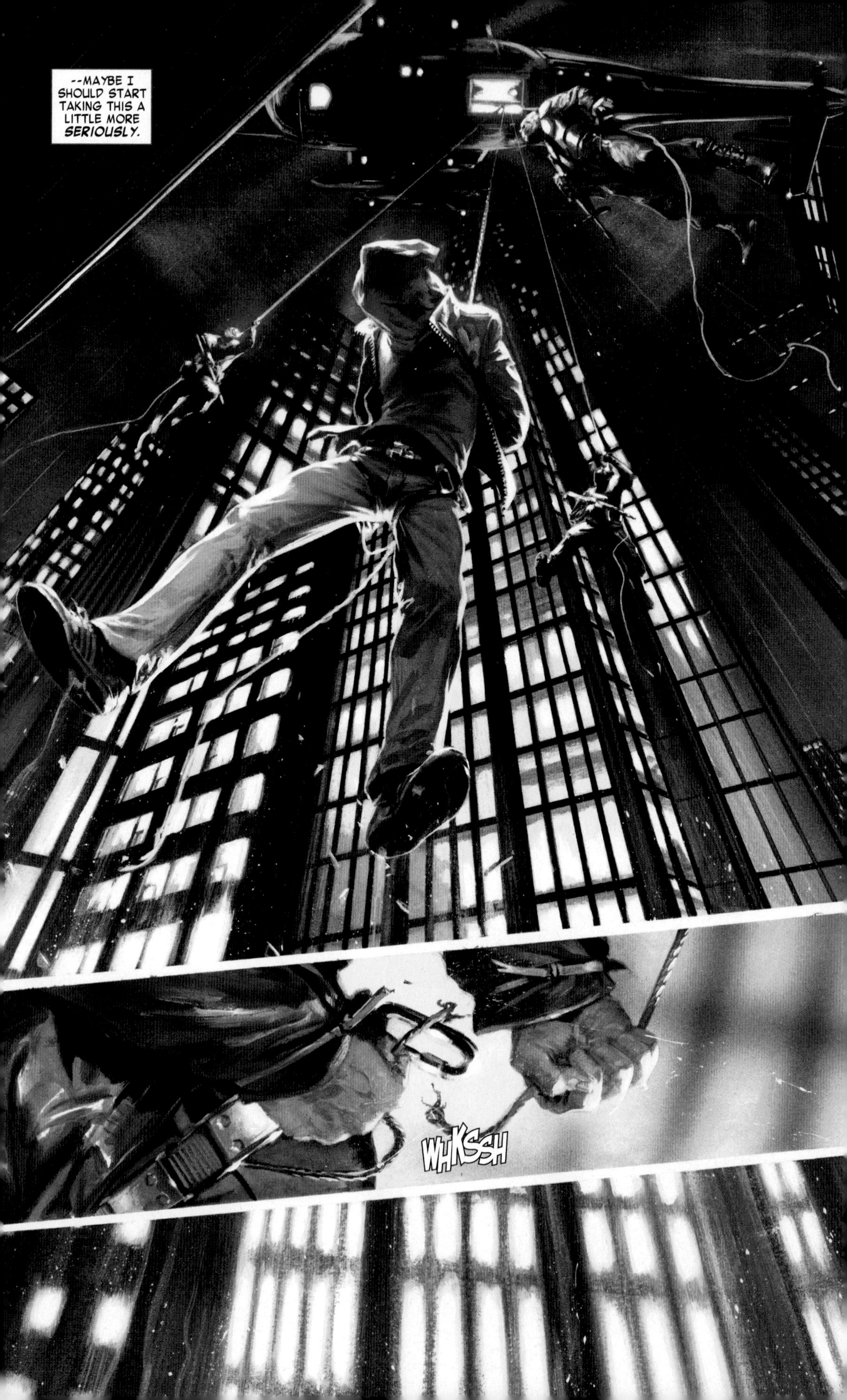
--MAYBE I SHOULD START TAKING THIS A LITTLE MORE SERIOUSLY.
WHKSSH

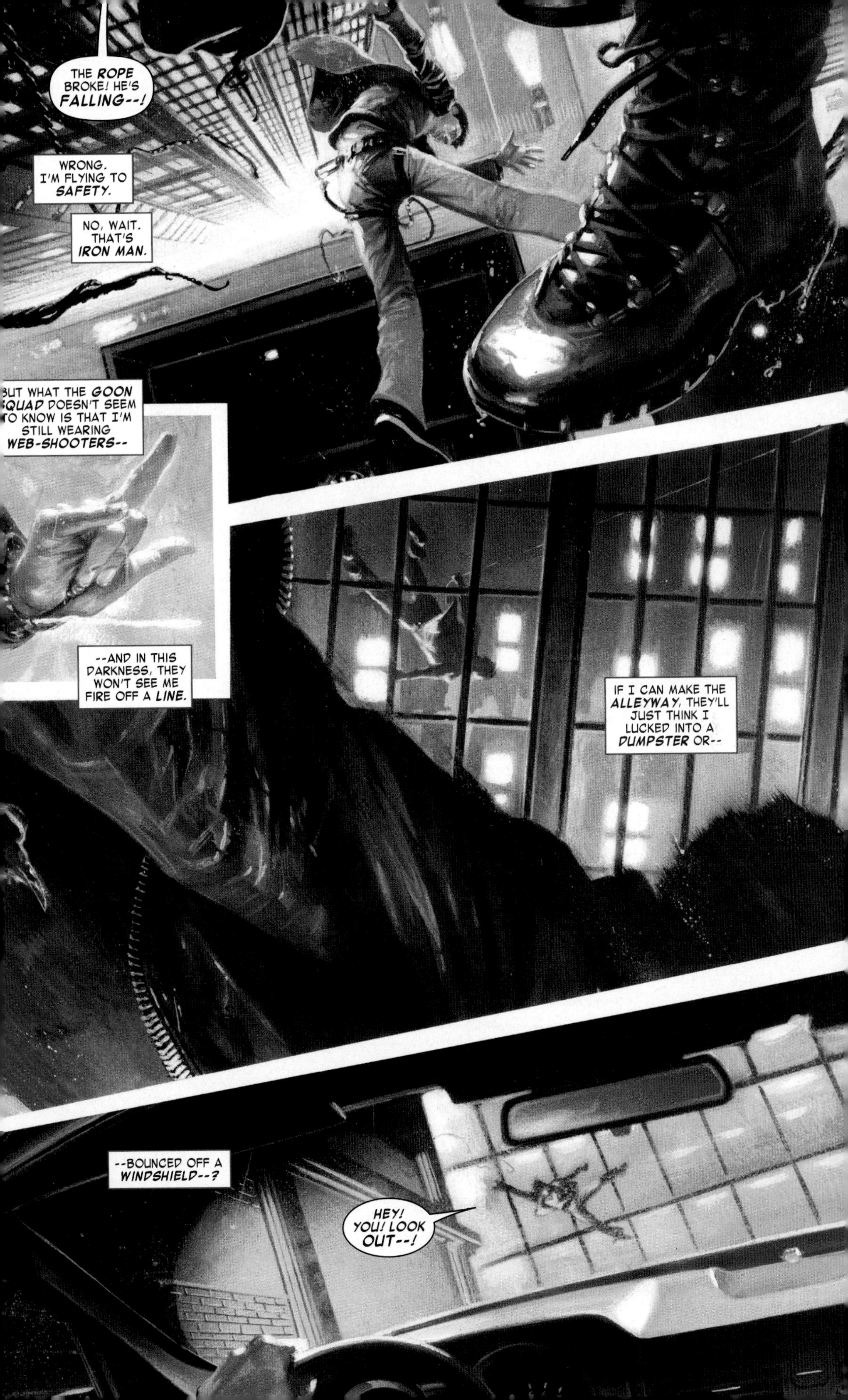
THE ROPE BROKE! HE'S FALLING--!
WRONG. I'M FLYING TO SAFETY.
NO, WAIT. THAT'S IRON MAN.
BUT WHAT THE GOON SQUAD DOESN'T SEEM TO KNOW IS THAT I'M STILL WEARING WEB-SHOOTERS--
--AND IN THIS DARKNESS, THEY WON'T SEE ME FIRE OFF A LINE.
IF I CAN MAKE THE ALLEYWAY, THEY'LL JUST THINK I LUCKED INTO A DUMPSTER OR--
--BOUNCED OFF A WINDSHIELD--?
HEY! YOU! LOOK OUT--!

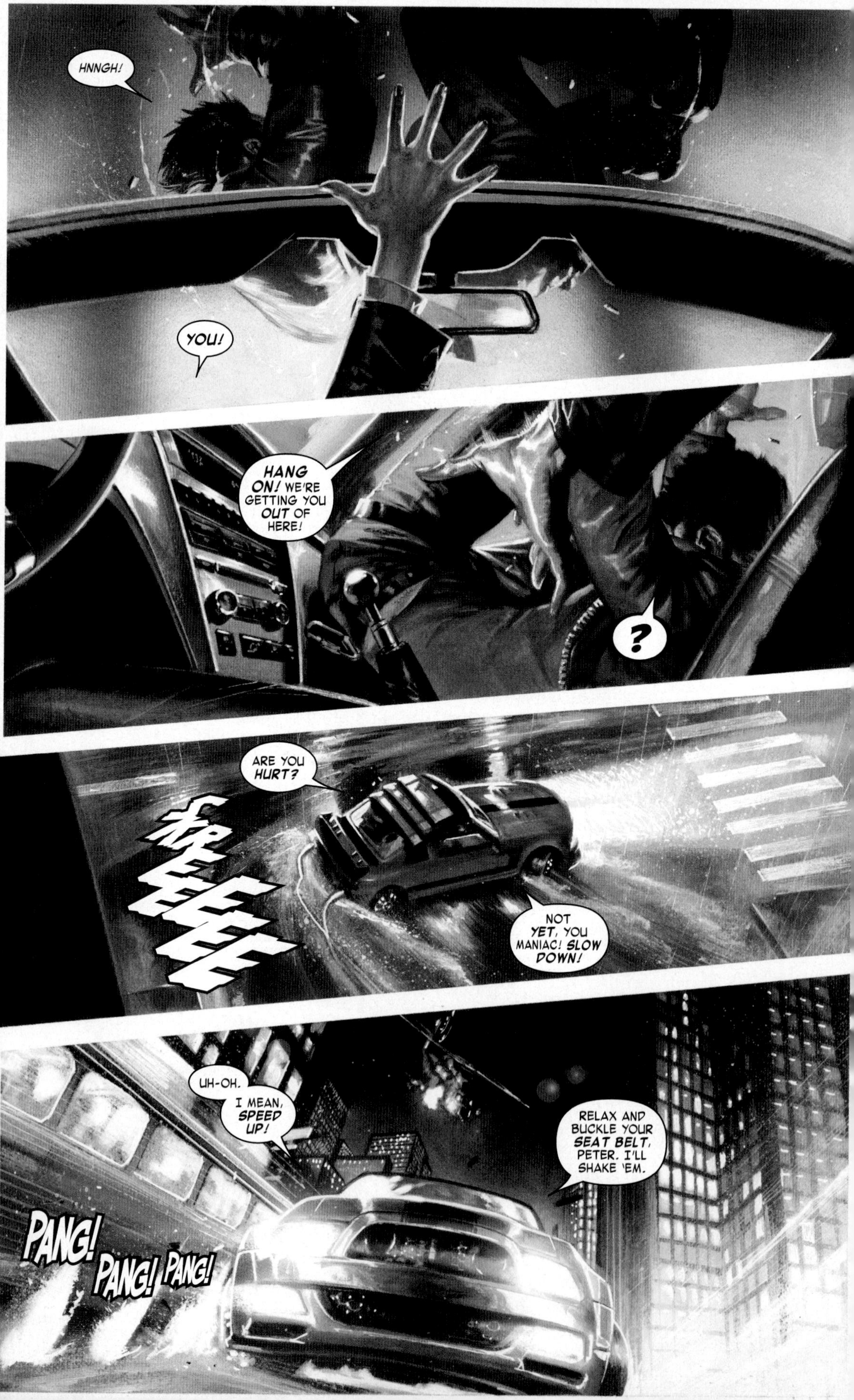
HNNGH!
YOU!
HANG ON! WE'RE GETTING YOU OUT OF HERE!
?
ARE YOU HURT?
SKREEEEE
NOT YET, YOU MANIAC! SLOW DOWN!
UH-OH.
I MEAN, SPEED UP!
RELAX AND BUCKLE YOUR SEAT BELT, PETER. I'LL SHAKE 'EM.
PANG! PANG! PANG!

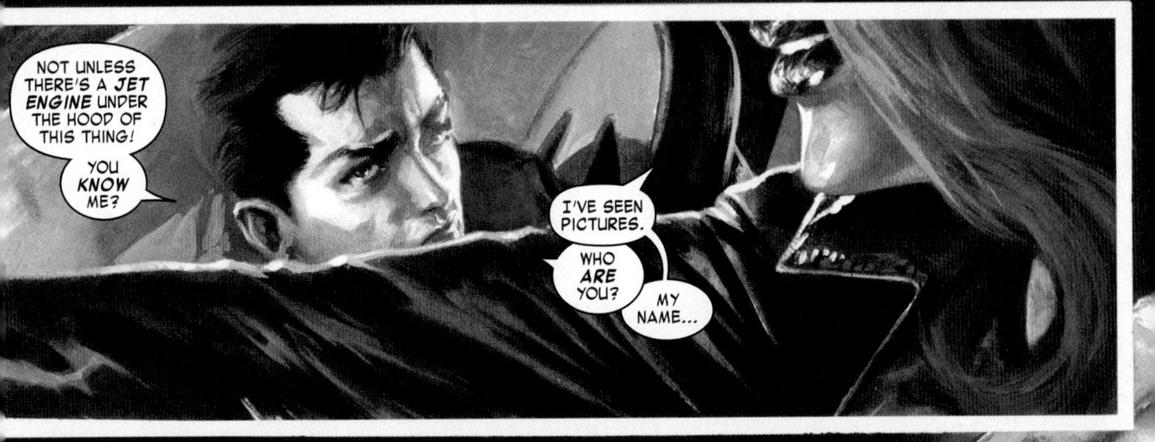
NOT UNLESS THERE'S A JET ENGINE UNDER THE HOOD OF THIS THING!
YOU KNOW ME?
I'VE SEEN PICTURES.
WHO ARE YOU?
MY NAME...

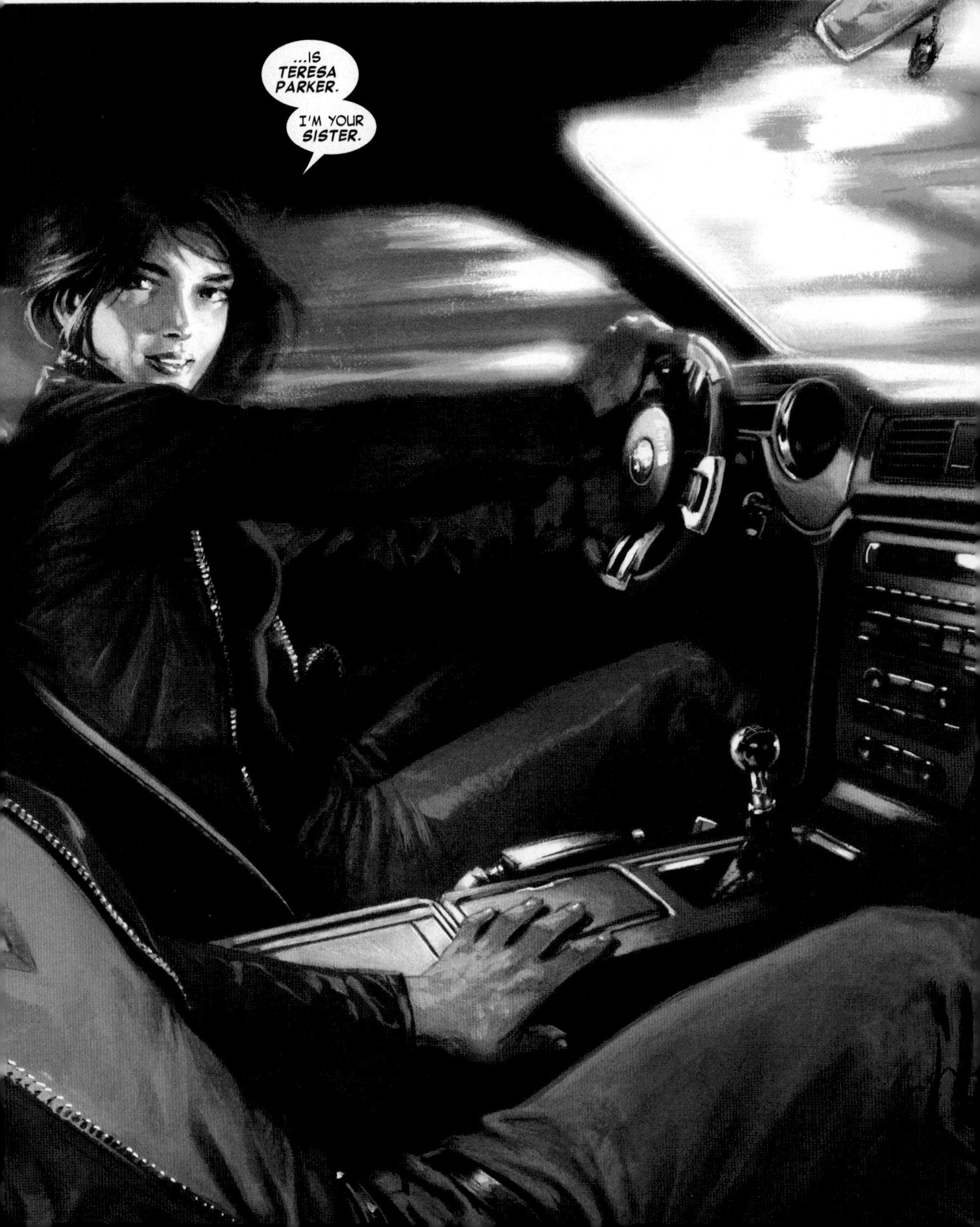
...IS TERESA PARKER.
I'M YOUR SISTER.

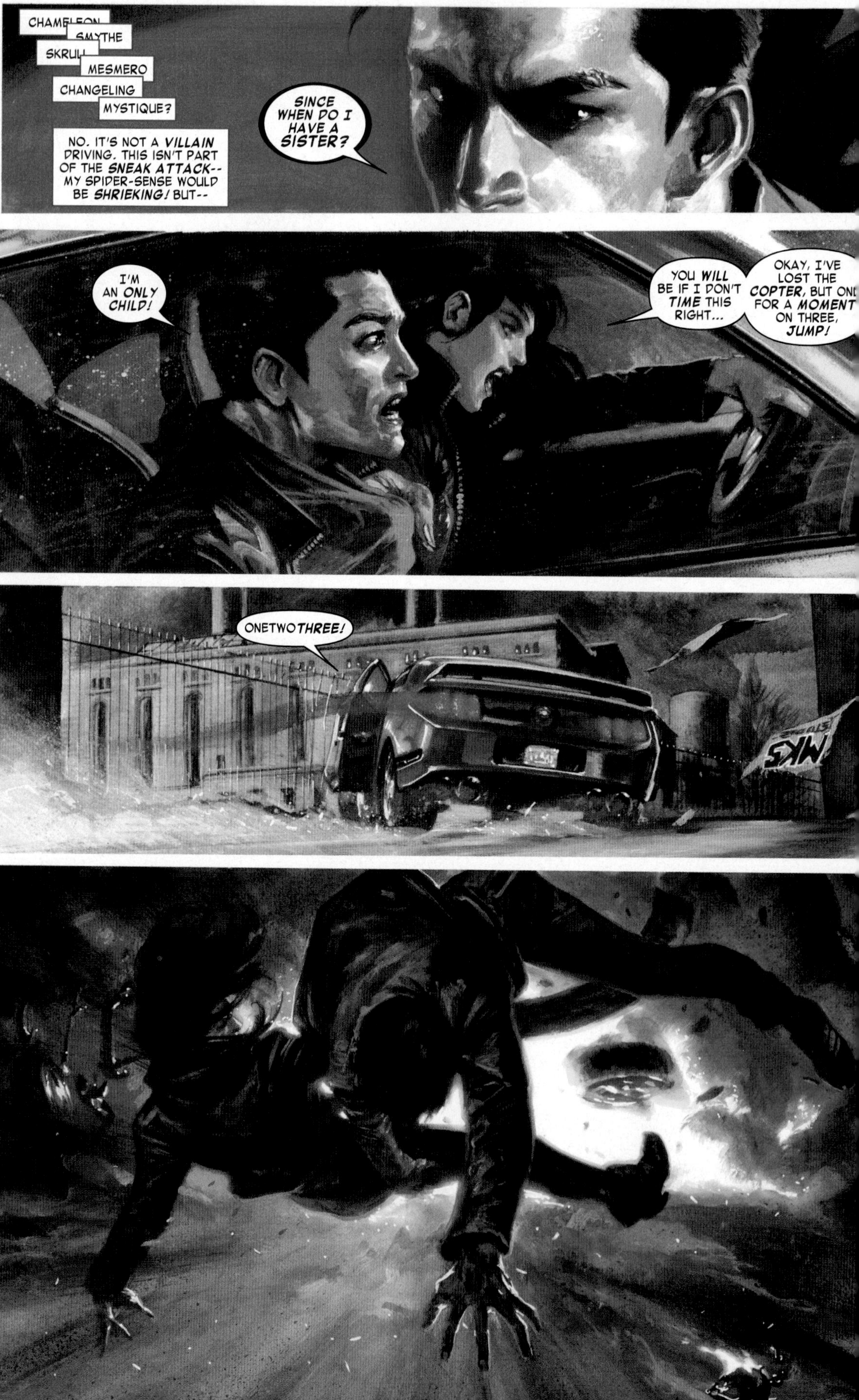
CHAMELEON
SMYTHE
SKRULL
MESMERO
CHANGELING
MYSTIQUE?
NO. IT'S NOT A VILLAIN DRIVING. THIS ISN'T PART OF THE SNEAK ATTACK-- MY SPIDER-SENSE WOULD BE SHRIEKING! BUT--
SINCE WHEN DO I HAVE A SISTER?
I'M AN ONLY CHILD!
YOU WILL BE IF I DON'T TIME THIS RIGHT...
OKAY, I'VE LOST THE COPTER, BUT ONL FOR A MOMENT ON THREE, JUMP!
ONETWOTHREE!

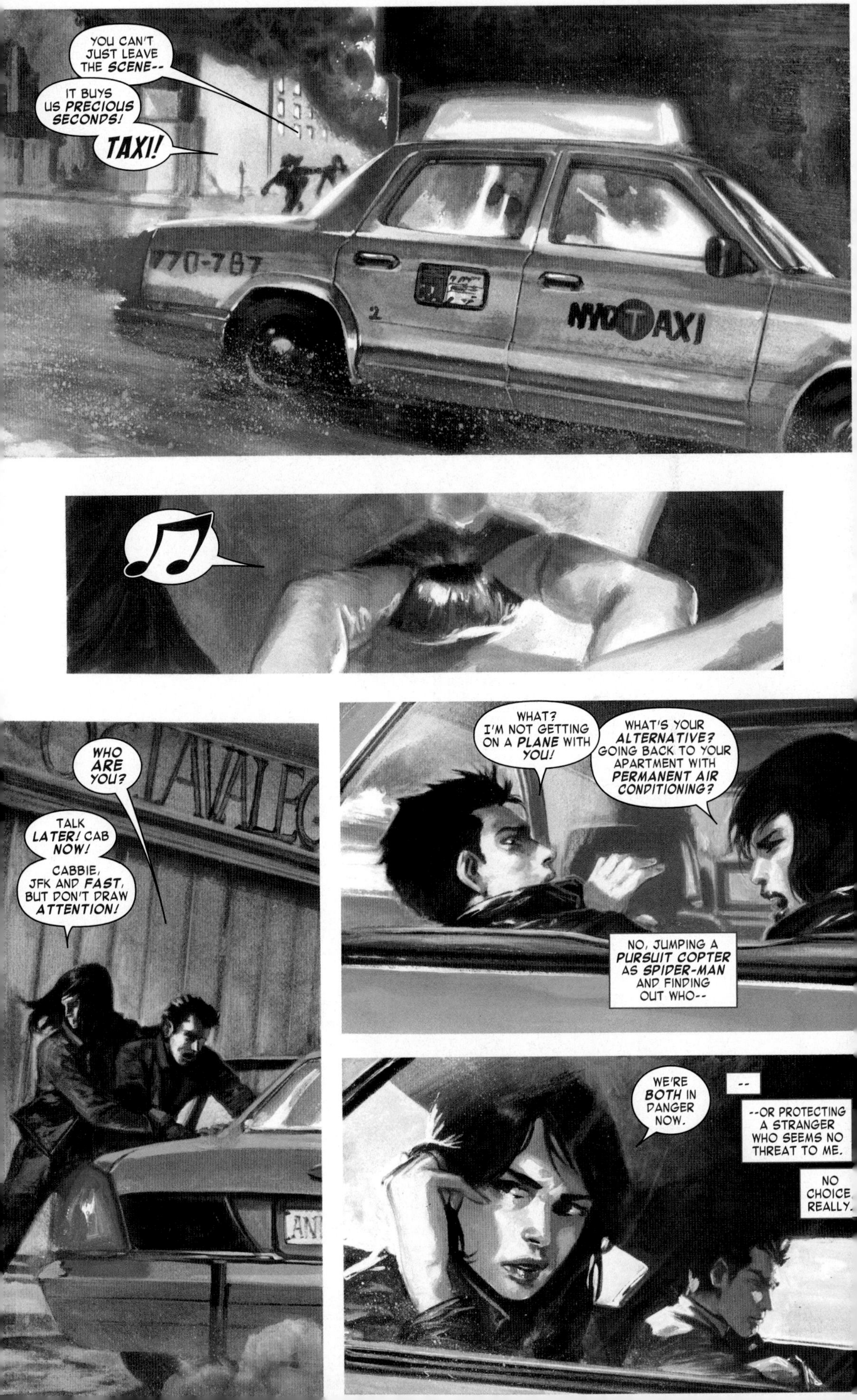
YOU CAN'T JUST LEAVE THE SCENE--
IT BUYS US PRECIOUS SECONDS!
TAXI!
770-787
NYC TAXI
WHO ARE YOU?
TALK LATER! CAB NOW!
CABBIE, JFK AND FAST, BUT DON'T DRAW ATTENTION!
WHAT? I'M NOT GETTING ON A PLANE WITH YOU!
WHAT'S YOUR ALTERNATIVE? GOING BACK TO YOUR APARTMENT WITH PERMANENT AIR CONDITIONING?
NO, JUMPING A PURSUIT COPTER AS SPIDER-MAN AND FINDING OUT WHO--
WE'RE BOTH IN DANGER NOW.
--
--OR PROTECTING A STRANGER WHO SEEMS NO THREAT TO ME.
NO CHOICE, REALLY.

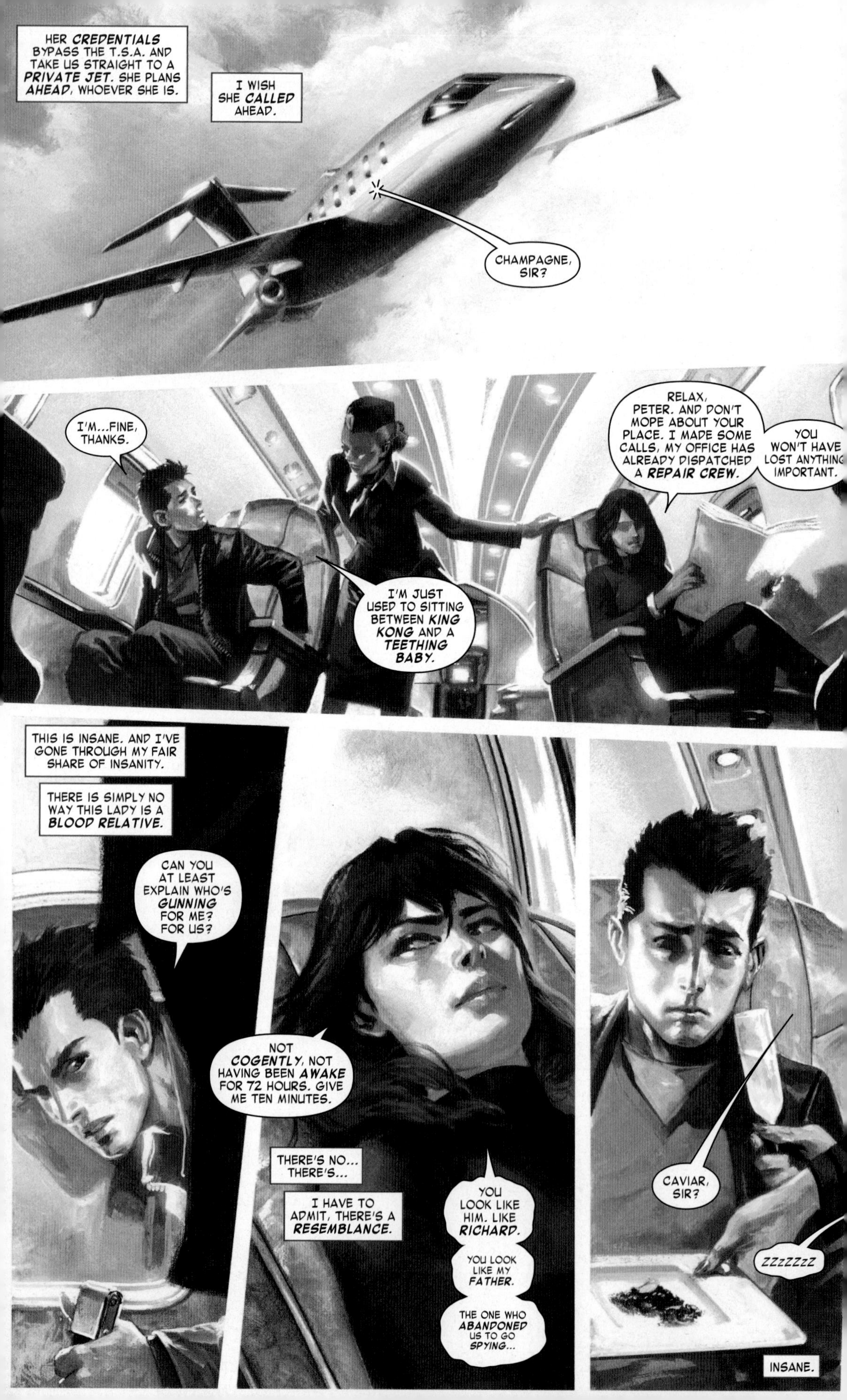
HER CREDENTIALS BYPASS THE T.S.A. AND TAKE US STRAIGHT TO A PRIVATE JET. SHE PLANS AHEAD, WHOEVER SHE IS.
I WISH SHE CALLED AHEAD.
CHAMPAGNE, SIR?
I'M...FINE, THANKS.
I'M JUST USED TO SITTING BETWEEN KING KONG AND A TEETHING BABY.
RELAX, PETER. AND DON'T MOPE ABOUT YOUR PLACE. I MADE SOME CALLS, MY OFFICE HAS ALREADY DISPATCHED A REPAIR CREW.
YOU WON'T HAVE LOST ANYTHING IMPORTANT.
THIS IS INSANE. AND I'VE GONE THROUGH MY FAIR SHARE OF INSANITY.
THERE IS SIMPLY NO WAY THIS LADY IS A BLOOD RELATIVE.
CAN YOU AT LEAST EXPLAIN WHO'S GUNNING FOR ME? FOR US?
NOT COGENTLY, NOT HAVING BEEN AWAKE FOR 72 HOURS. GIVE ME TEN MINUTES.
THERE'S NO... THERE'S...
I HAVE TO ADMIT, THERE'S A RESEMBLANCE.
YOU LOOK LIKE HIM. LIKE RICHARD.
YOU LOOK LIKE MY FATHER.
THE ONE WHO ABANDONED US TO GO SPYING...
CAVIAR, SIR?
ZZZZZZZ
INSANE.

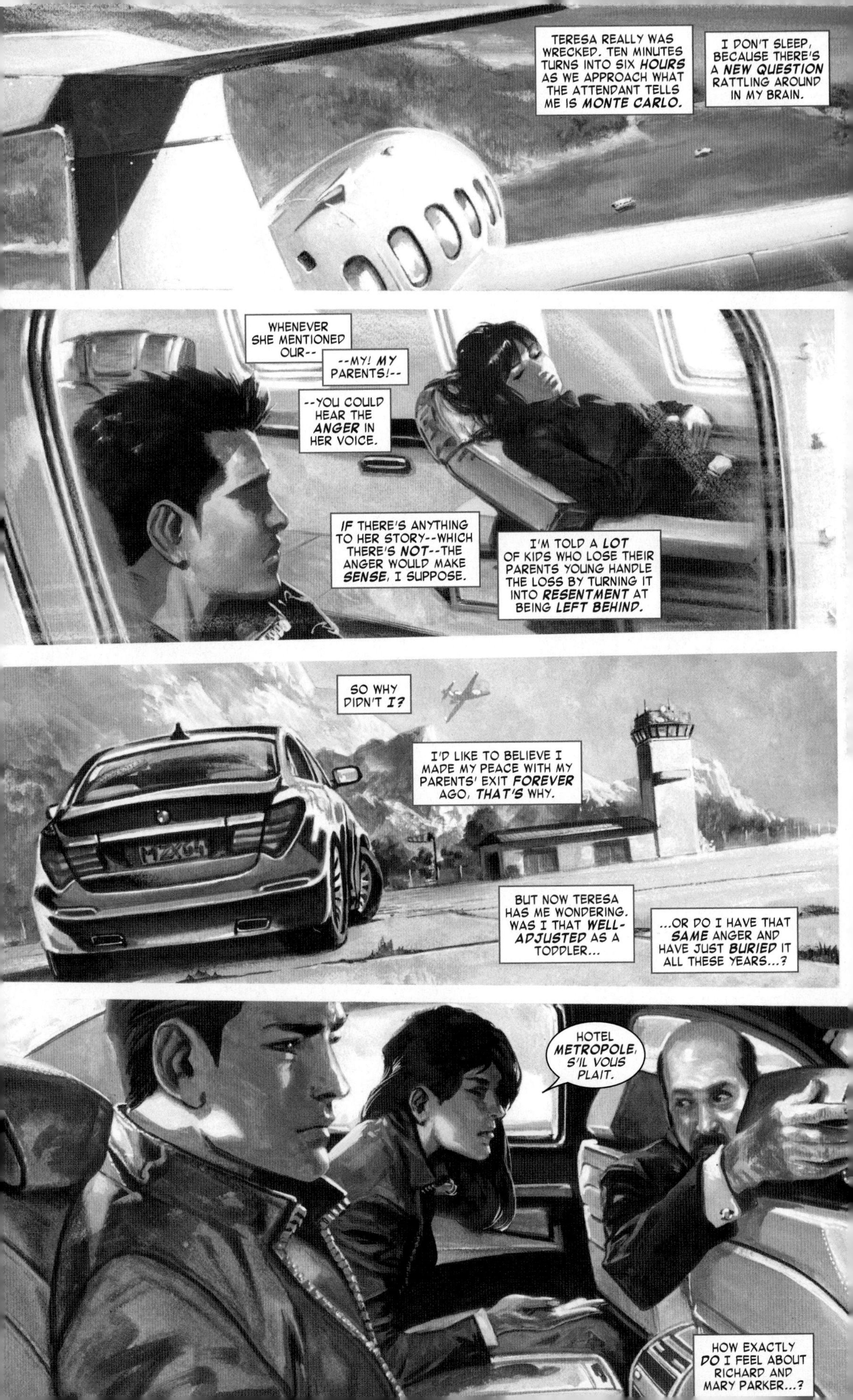

TERESA REALLY WAS WRECKED. TEN MINUTES TURNS INTO SIX HOURS AS WE APPROACH WHAT THE ATTENDANT TELLS ME IS MONTE CARLO.
I DON'T SLEEP, BECAUSE THERE'S A NEW QUESTION RATTLING AROUND IN MY BRAIN.
WHENEVER SHE MENTIONED OUR--
--MY! MY PARENTS!--
--YOU COULD HEAR THE ANGER IN HER VOICE.
IF THERE'S ANYTHING TO HER STORY--WHICH THERE'S NOT--THE ANGER WOULD MAKE SENSE, I SUPPOSE.
I'M TOLD A LOT OF KIDS WHO LOSE THEIR PARENTS YOUNG HANDLE THE LOSS BY TURNING IT INTO RESENTMENT AT BEING LEFT BEHIND.
SO WHY DIDN'T I?
I'D LIKE TO BELIEVE I MADE MY PEACE WITH MY PARENTS' EXIT FOREVER AGO, THAT'S WHY.
BUT NOW TERESA HAS ME WONDERING. WAS I THAT WELL-ADJUSTED AS A TODDLER...
...OR DO I HAVE THAT SAME ANGER AND HAVE JUST BURIED IT ALL THESE YEARS...?
HOTEL METROPOLE, S'IL VOUS PLAIT.
HOW EXACTLY DO I FEEL ABOUT RICHARD AND MARY PARKER...?

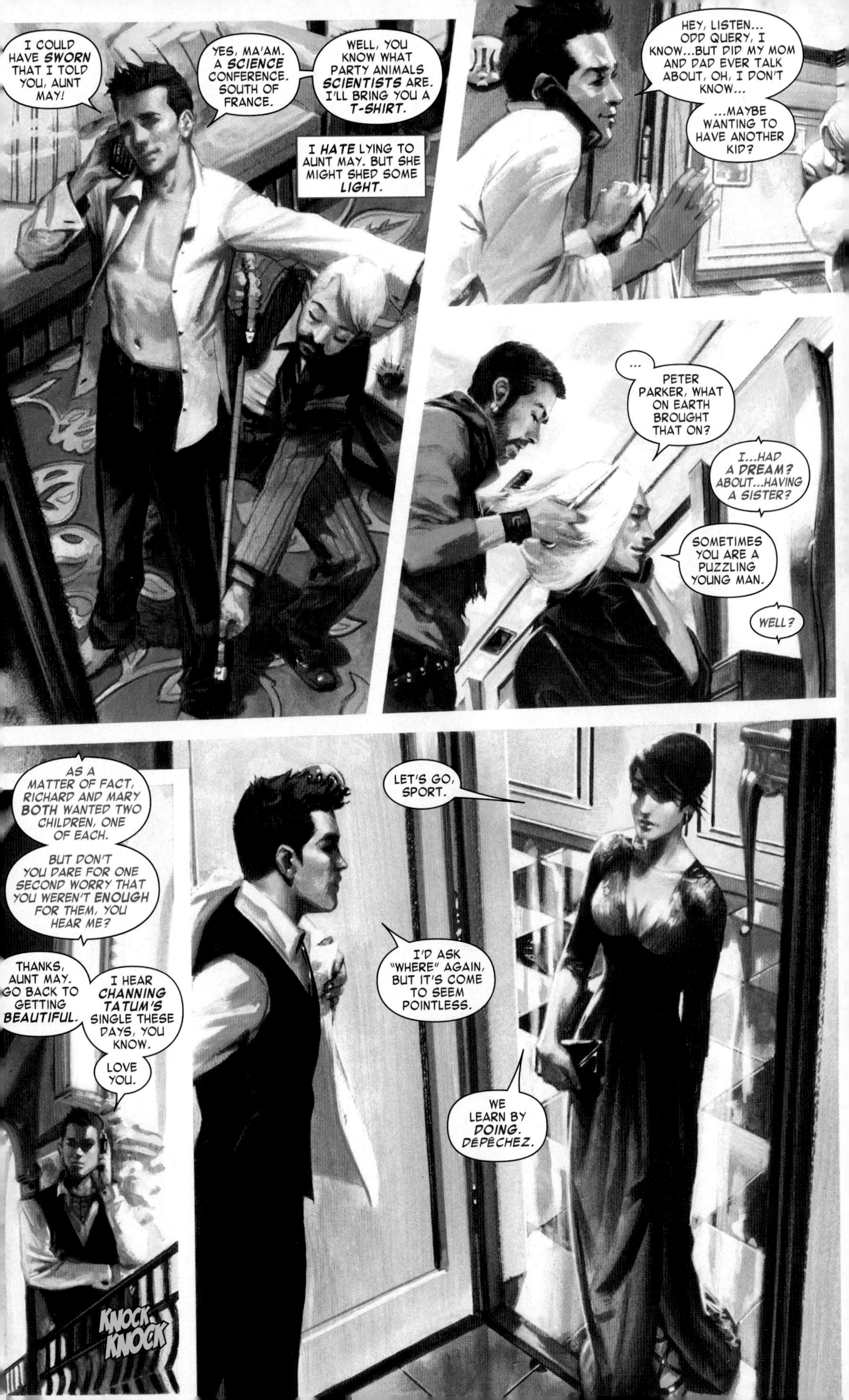
I COULD HAVE **SWORN** THAT I TOLD YOU, AUNT MAY!
YES, MA'AM. A **SCIENCE** CONFERENCE. SOUTH OF FRANCE.
WELL, YOU KNOW WHAT PARTY ANIMALS **SCIENTISTS** ARE. I'LL BRING YOU A **T-SHIRT**.
I **HATE** LYING TO AUNT MAY. BUT SHE MIGHT SHED SOME **LIGHT**.
HEY, LISTEN... ODD QUERY, I KNOW...BUT DID MY MOM AND DAD EVER TALK ABOUT, OH, I DON'T KNOW...
...MAYBE WANTING TO HAVE ANOTHER KID?
...
PETER PARKER, WHAT ON EARTH BROUGHT THAT ON?
I...HAD A **DREAM?** ABOUT...HAVING A SISTER?
SOMETIMES YOU ARE A PUZZLING YOUNG MAN.
WELL?
AS A MATTER OF FACT, RICHARD AND MARY **BOTH** WANTED TWO CHILDREN, ONE OF EACH.
BUT DON'T YOU DARE FOR ONE SECOND WORRY THAT YOU WEREN'T **ENOUGH** FOR THEM, YOU HEAR ME?
THANKS, AUNT MAY. GO BACK TO GETTING **BEAUTIFUL**.
I HEAR **CHANNING TATUM'S** SINGLE THESE DAYS, YOU KNOW.
LOVE YOU.
KNOCK KNOCK
LET'S GO, SPORT.
I'D ASK "WHERE" AGAIN, BUT IT'S COME TO SEEM POINTLESS.
WE LEARN BY **DOING**. DÉPÊCHEZ.

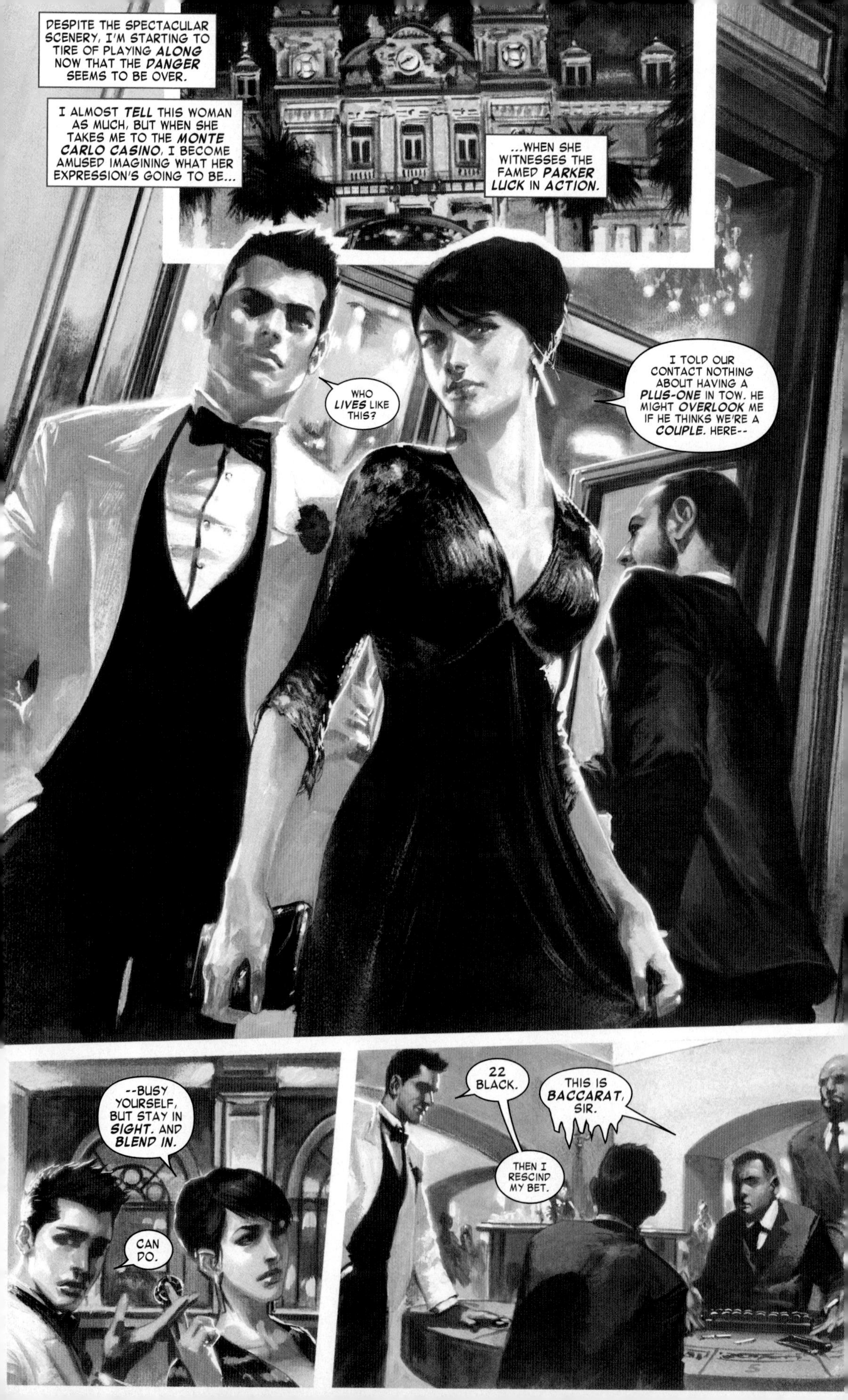
DESPITE THE SPECTACULAR SCENERY, I'M STARTING TO TIRE OF PLAYING ALONG NOW THAT THE DANGER SEEMS TO BE OVER.
I ALMOST TELL THIS WOMAN AS MUCH, BUT WHEN SHE TAKES ME TO THE MONTE CARLO CASINO, I BECOME AMUSED IMAGINING WHAT HER EXPRESSION'S GOING TO BE...
...WHEN SHE WITNESSES THE FAMED PARKER LUCK IN ACTION.
WHO LIVES LIKE THIS?
I TOLD OUR CONTACT NOTHING ABOUT HAVING A PLUS-ONE IN TOW. HE MIGHT OVERLOOK ME IF HE THINKS WE'RE A COUPLE. HERE--
--BUSY YOURSELF, BUT STAY IN SIGHT. AND BLEND IN.
CAN DO.
22 BLACK.
THIS IS BACCARAT, SIR.
THEN I RESCIND MY BET.

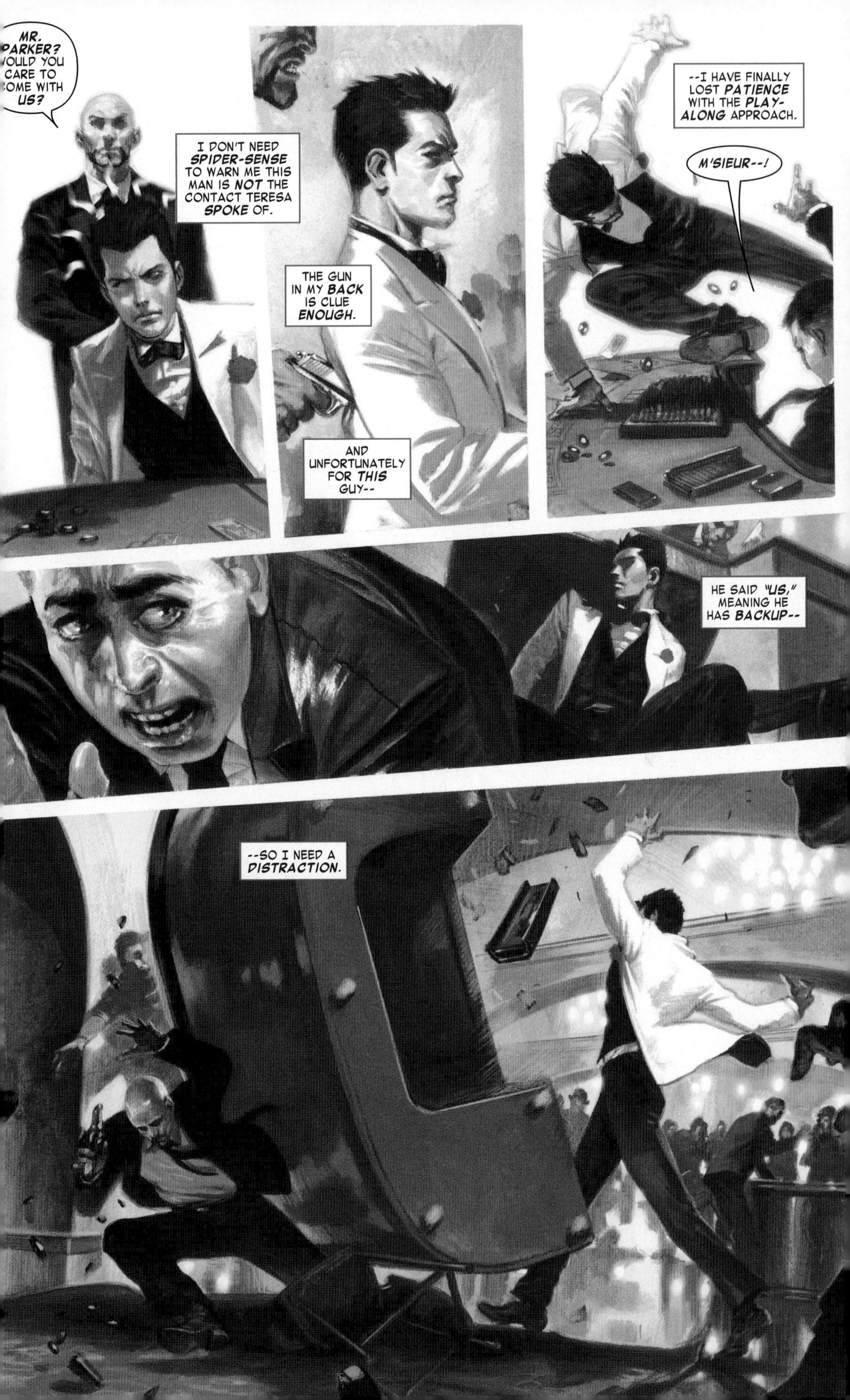
MR. PARKER? WOULD YOU CARE TO COME WITH US?
I DON'T NEED SPIDER-SENSE TO WARN ME THIS MAN IS NOT THE CONTACT TERESA SPOKE OF.
THE GUN IN MY BACK IS CLUE ENOUGH.
AND UNFORTUNATELY FOR THIS GUY--
--I HAVE FINALLY LOST PATIENCE WITH THE PLAY-ALONG APPROACH.
M'SIEUR--!
HE SAID "US," MEANING HE HAS BACKUP--
--SO I NEED A DISTRACTION.

ZE PARKAIRS-- --ZEY ARE UNDAIR MY PROTECTI-OWN!

OH, MAN, I SURE HOPE THAT ACCENT FOOLS *SOMEBODY.*

PETER! PETER, *WHERE ARE YOU?*

GUESS SO.

NOT *EVERYONE'S* WIGGED OUT. *TRENCHCOAT* HERE IS UNNATURALLY CALM, FOR INSTANCE.

I SURE HOPE IT'S *NICK FURY* ASKING ME TO JOIN THE *AVENGERS,* 'CAUSE IF *NOT--*

11 28   0 32 15 19 4 21 2

--THIS IS GONNA GET *UGLY.*

BECAUSE I *RECOGNIZE* THAT HUMAN WHIRLWIND.

HE'S A *SUPER-POWERED MERCENARY--*

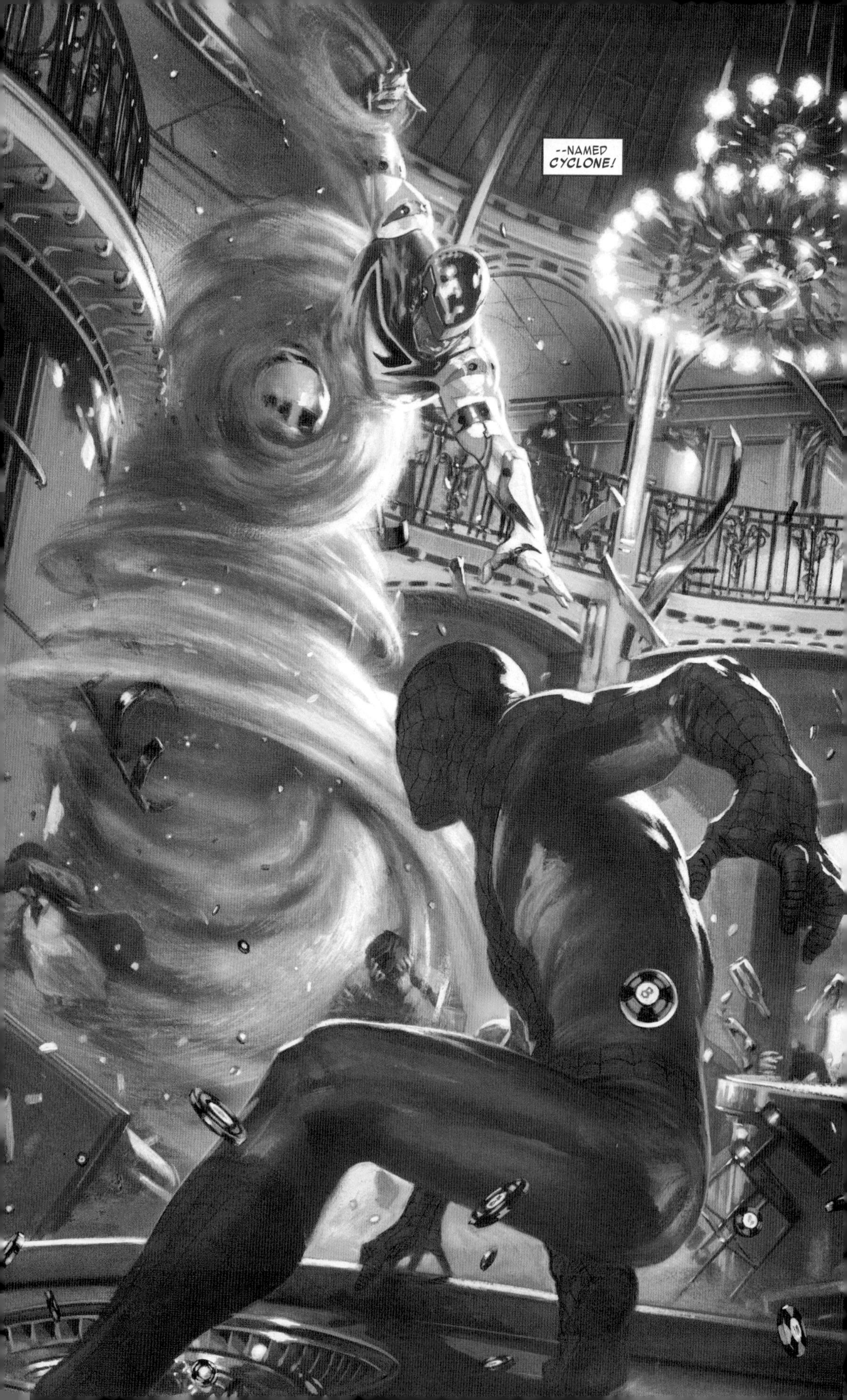
--NAMED CYCLONE!

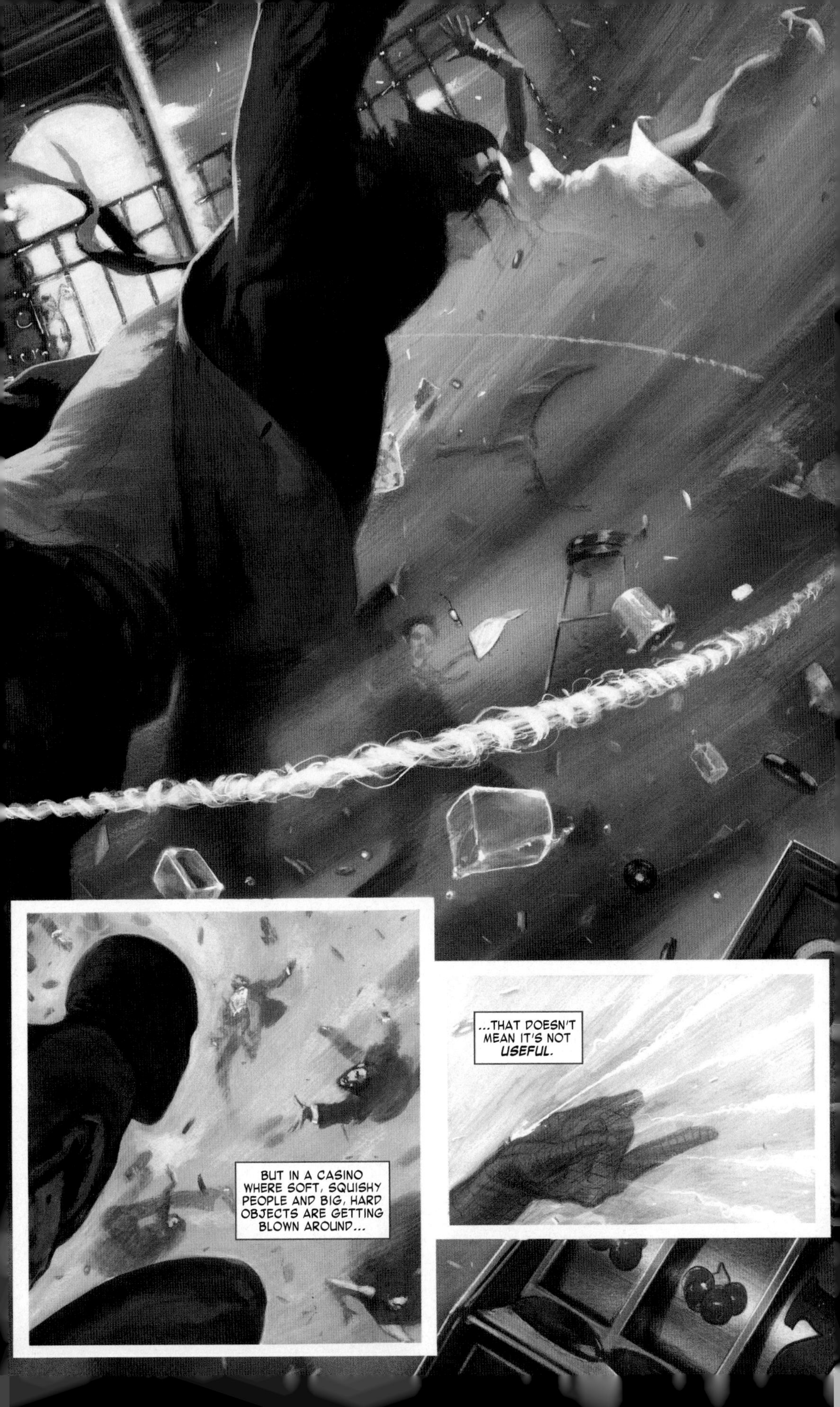
BUT IN A CASINO WHERE SOFT, SQUISHY PEOPLE AND BIG, HARD OBJECTS ARE GETTING BLOWN AROUND...
...THAT DOESN'T MEAN IT'S NOT USEFUL.

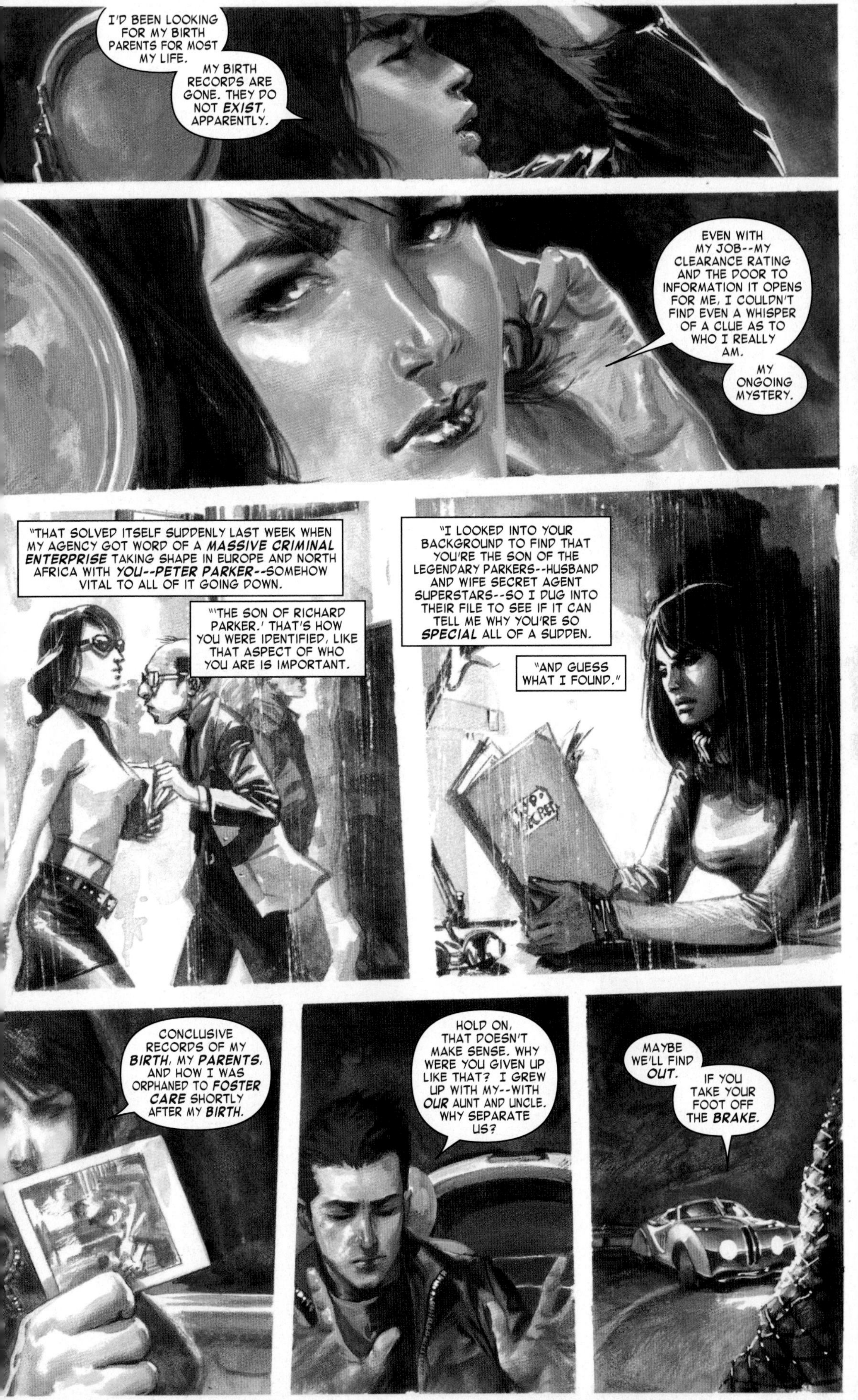
I'D BEEN LOOKING FOR MY BIRTH PARENTS FOR MOST MY LIFE.
MY BIRTH RECORDS ARE GONE. THEY DO NOT EXIST, APPARENTLY.
EVEN WITH MY JOB--MY CLEARANCE RATING AND THE DOOR TO INFORMATION IT OPENS FOR ME, I COULDN'T FIND EVEN A WHISPER OF A CLUE AS TO WHO I REALLY AM.
MY ONGOING MYSTERY.
"THAT SOLVED ITSELF SUDDENLY LAST WEEK WHEN MY AGENCY GOT WORD OF A MASSIVE CRIMINAL ENTERPRISE TAKING SHAPE IN EUROPE AND NORTH AFRICA WITH YOU--PETER PARKER--SOMEHOW VITAL TO ALL OF IT GOING DOWN.
"'THE SON OF RICHARD PARKER.' THAT'S HOW YOU WERE IDENTIFIED, LIKE THAT ASPECT OF WHO YOU ARE IS IMPORTANT.
"I LOOKED INTO YOUR BACKGROUND TO FIND THAT YOU'RE THE SON OF THE LEGENDARY PARKERS--HUSBAND AND WIFE SECRET AGENT SUPERSTARS--SO I DUG INTO THEIR FILE TO SEE IF IT CAN TELL ME WHY YOU'RE SO SPECIAL ALL OF A SUDDEN.
"AND GUESS WHAT I FOUND."
CONCLUSIVE RECORDS OF MY BIRTH, MY PARENTS, AND HOW I WAS ORPHANED TO FOSTER CARE SHORTLY AFTER MY BIRTH.
HOLD ON, THAT DOESN'T MAKE SENSE. WHY WERE YOU GIVEN UP LIKE THAT? I GREW UP WITH MY--WITH OUR AUNT AND UNCLE. WHY SEPARATE US?
MAYBE WE'LL FIND OUT.
IF YOU TAKE YOUR FOOT OFF THE BRAKE.

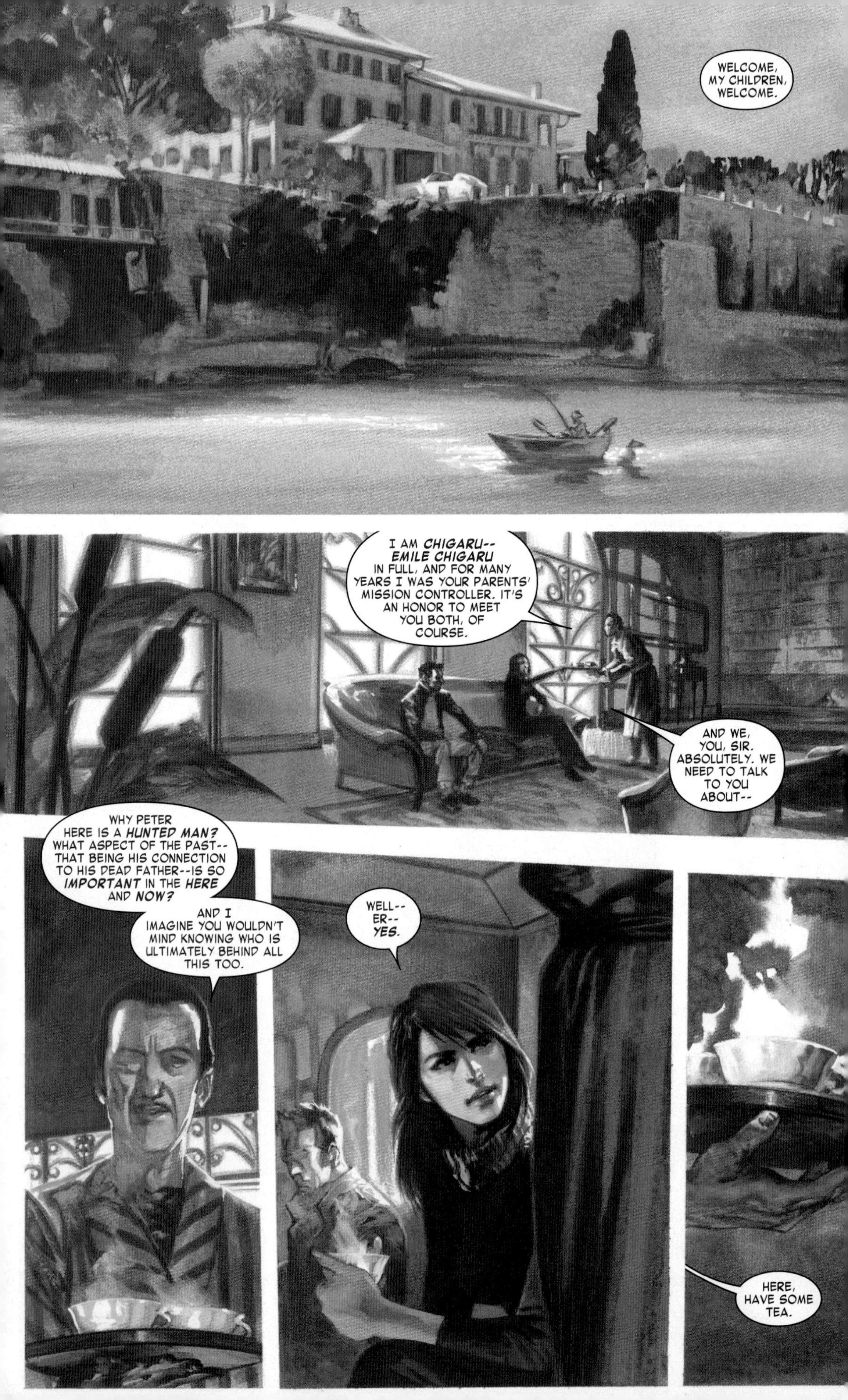
WELCOME, MY CHILDREN, WELCOME.
I AM CHIGARU-- EMILE CHIGARU IN FULL, AND FOR MANY YEARS I WAS YOUR PARENTS' MISSION CONTROLLER. IT'S AN HONOR TO MEET YOU BOTH, OF COURSE.
AND WE, YOU, SIR. ABSOLUTELY. WE NEED TO TALK TO YOU ABOUT--
WHY PETER HERE IS A HUNTED MAN? WHAT ASPECT OF THE PAST-- THAT BEING HIS CONNECTION TO HIS DEAD FATHER--IS SO IMPORTANT IN THE HERE AND NOW?
AND I IMAGINE YOU WOULDN'T MIND KNOWING WHO IS ULTIMATELY BEHIND ALL THIS TOO.
WELL-- ER-- YES.
HERE, HAVE SOME TEA.

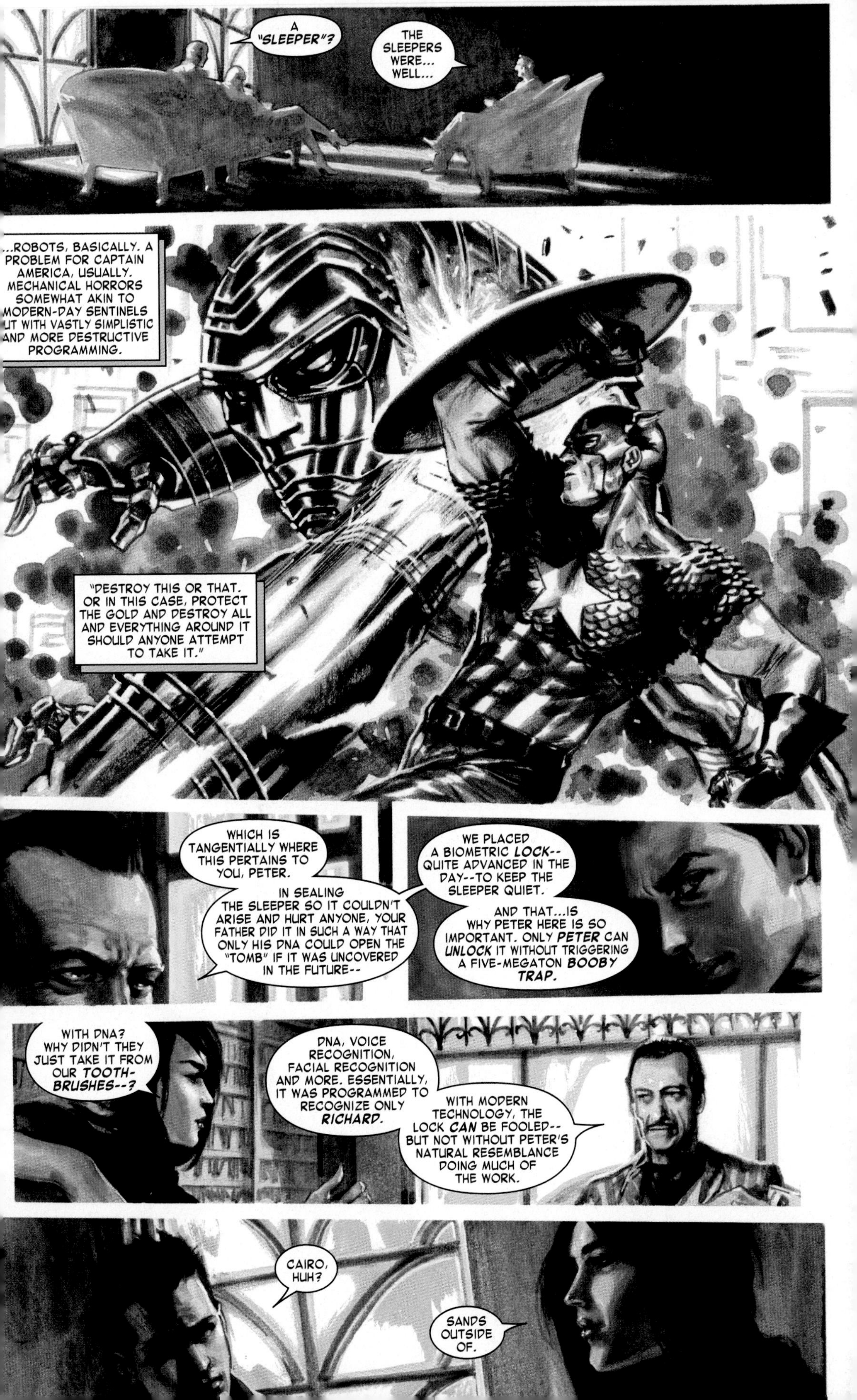
A "SLEEPER"?
THE SLEEPERS WERE... WELL...
...ROBOTS, BASICALLY. A PROBLEM FOR CAPTAIN AMERICA, USUALLY. MECHANICAL HORRORS SOMEWHAT AKIN TO MODERN-DAY SENTINELS BUT WITH VASTLY SIMPLISTIC AND MORE DESTRUCTIVE PROGRAMMING.
"DESTROY THIS OR THAT. OR IN THIS CASE, PROTECT THE GOLD AND DESTROY ALL AND EVERYTHING AROUND IT SHOULD ANYONE ATTEMPT TO TAKE IT."
WHICH IS TANGENTIALLY WHERE THIS PERTAINS TO YOU, PETER.
IN SEALING THE SLEEPER SO IT COULDN'T ARISE AND HURT ANYONE, YOUR FATHER DID IT IN SUCH A WAY THAT ONLY HIS DNA COULD OPEN THE "TOMB" IF IT WAS UNCOVERED IN THE FUTURE--
WE PLACED A BIOMETRIC LOCK-- QUITE ADVANCED IN THE DAY--TO KEEP THE SLEEPER QUIET.
AND THAT...IS WHY PETER HERE IS SO IMPORTANT. ONLY PETER CAN UNLOCK IT WITHOUT TRIGGERING A FIVE-MEGATON BOOBY TRAP.
WITH DNA? WHY DIDN'T THEY JUST TAKE IT FROM OUR TOOTH-BRUSHES--?
DNA, VOICE RECOGNITION, FACIAL RECOGNITION AND MORE. ESSENTIALLY, IT WAS PROGRAMMED TO RECOGNIZE ONLY RICHARD.
WITH MODERN TECHNOLOGY, THE LOCK CAN BE FOOLED-- BUT NOT WITHOUT PETER'S NATURAL RESEMBLANCE DOING MUCH OF THE WORK.
CAIRO, HUH?
SANDS OUTSIDE OF.

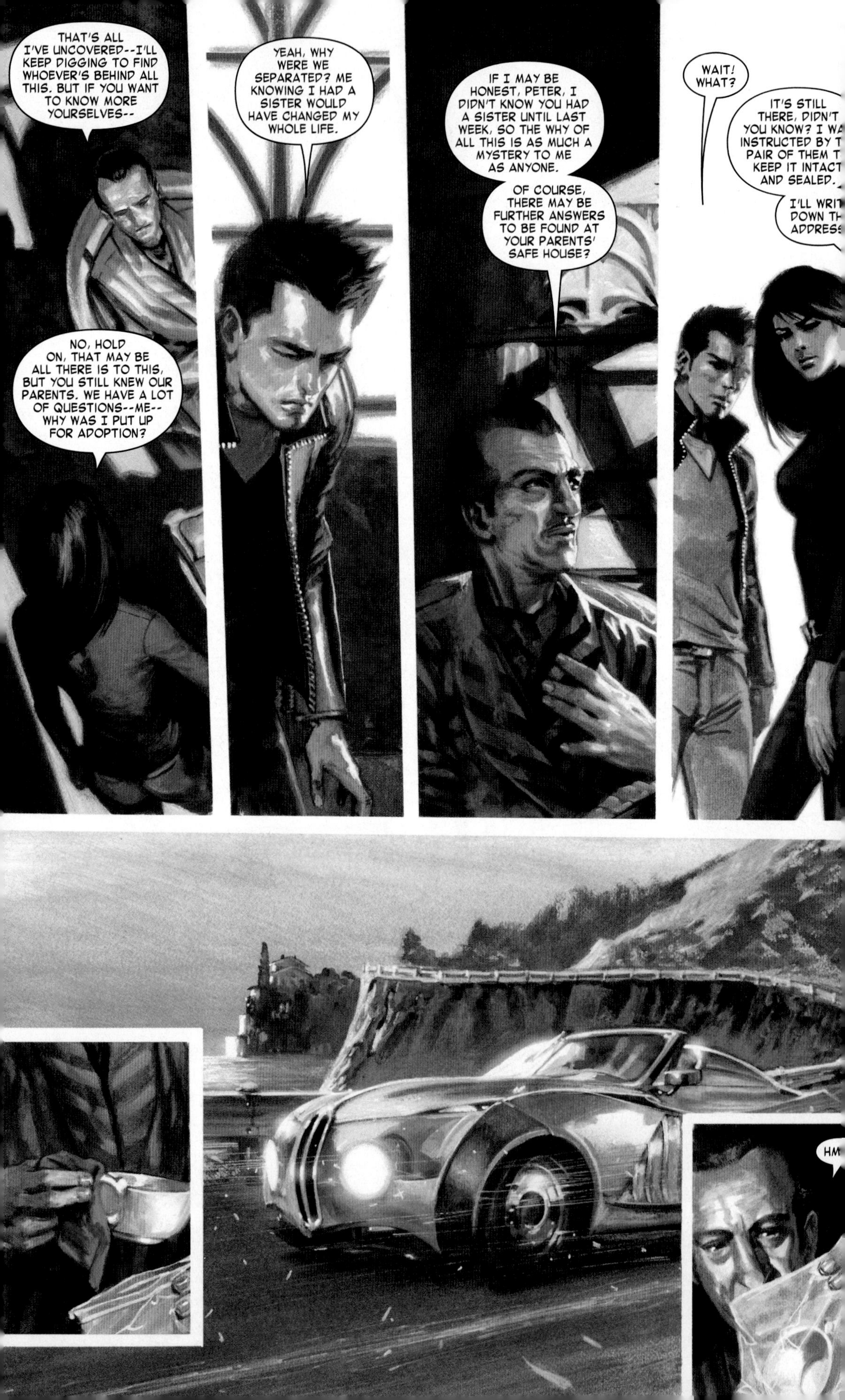
THAT'S ALL I'VE UNCOVERED--I'LL KEEP DIGGING TO FIND WHOEVER'S BEHIND ALL THIS. BUT IF YOU WANT TO KNOW MORE YOURSELVES--
NO, HOLD ON, THAT MAY BE ALL THERE IS TO THIS, BUT YOU STILL KNEW OUR PARENTS. WE HAVE A LOT OF QUESTIONS--ME--WHY WAS I PUT UP FOR ADOPTION?
YEAH, WHY WERE WE SEPARATED? ME KNOWING I HAD A SISTER WOULD HAVE CHANGED MY WHOLE LIFE.
IF I MAY BE HONEST, PETER, I DIDN'T KNOW YOU HAD A SISTER UNTIL LAST WEEK, SO THE WHY OF ALL THIS IS AS MUCH A MYSTERY TO ME AS ANYONE.
OF COURSE, THERE MAY BE FURTHER ANSWERS TO BE FOUND AT YOUR PARENTS' SAFE HOUSE?
WAIT! WHAT?
IT'S STILL THERE, DIDN'T YOU KNOW? I WA INSTRUCTED BY T PAIR OF THEM T KEEP IT INTACT AND SEALED.
I'LL WRIT DOWN TH ADDRESS
HM

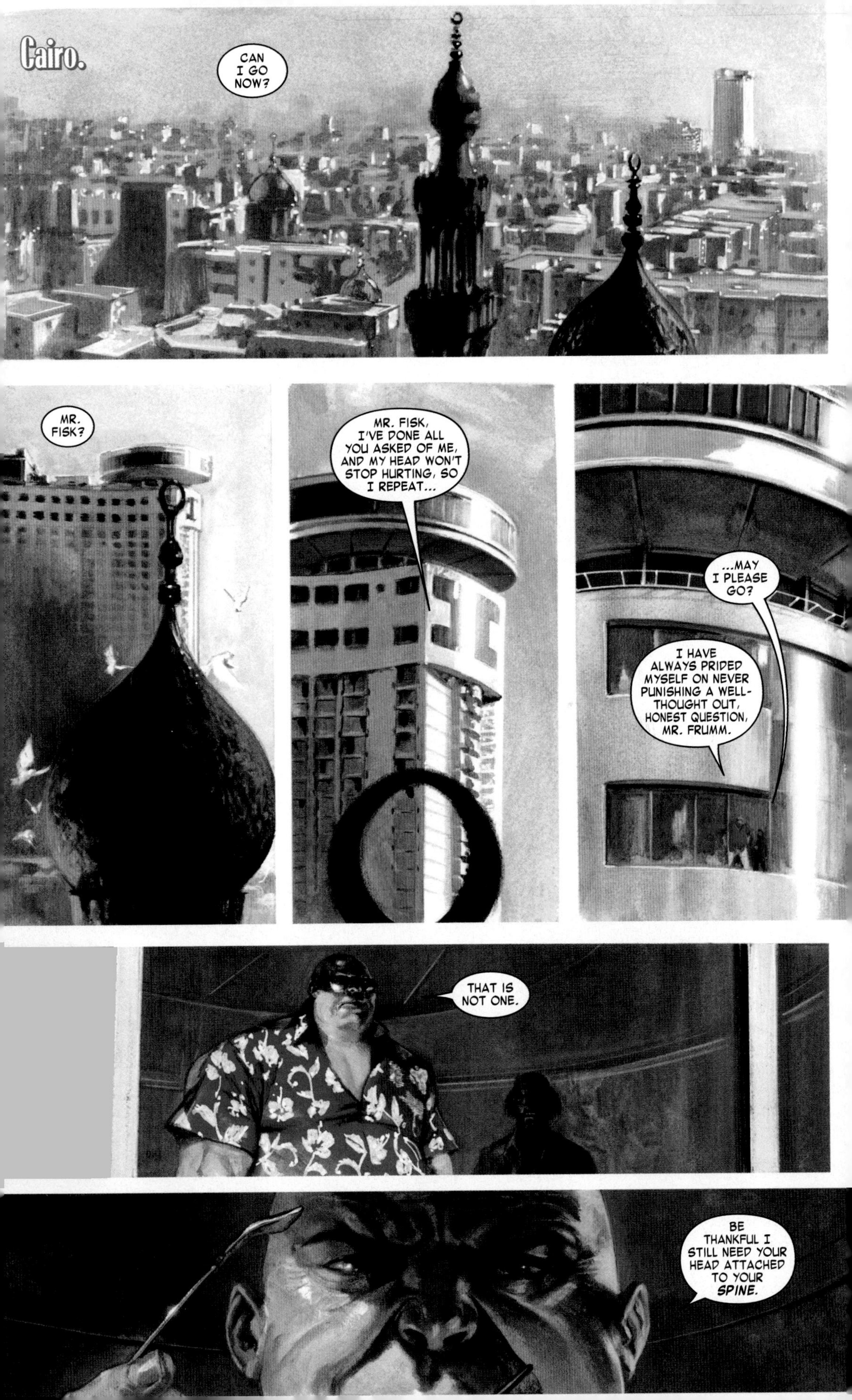
Cairo.
CAN I GO NOW?
MR. FISK?
MR. FISK, I'VE DONE ALL YOU ASKED OF ME, AND MY HEAD WON'T STOP HURTING, SO I REPEAT...
...MAY I PLEASE GO?
I HAVE ALWAYS PRIDED MYSELF ON NEVER PUNISHING A WELL-THOUGHT OUT, HONEST QUESTION, MR. FRUMM.
THAT IS NOT ONE.
BE THANKFUL I STILL NEED YOUR HEAD ATTACHED TO YOUR SPINE.

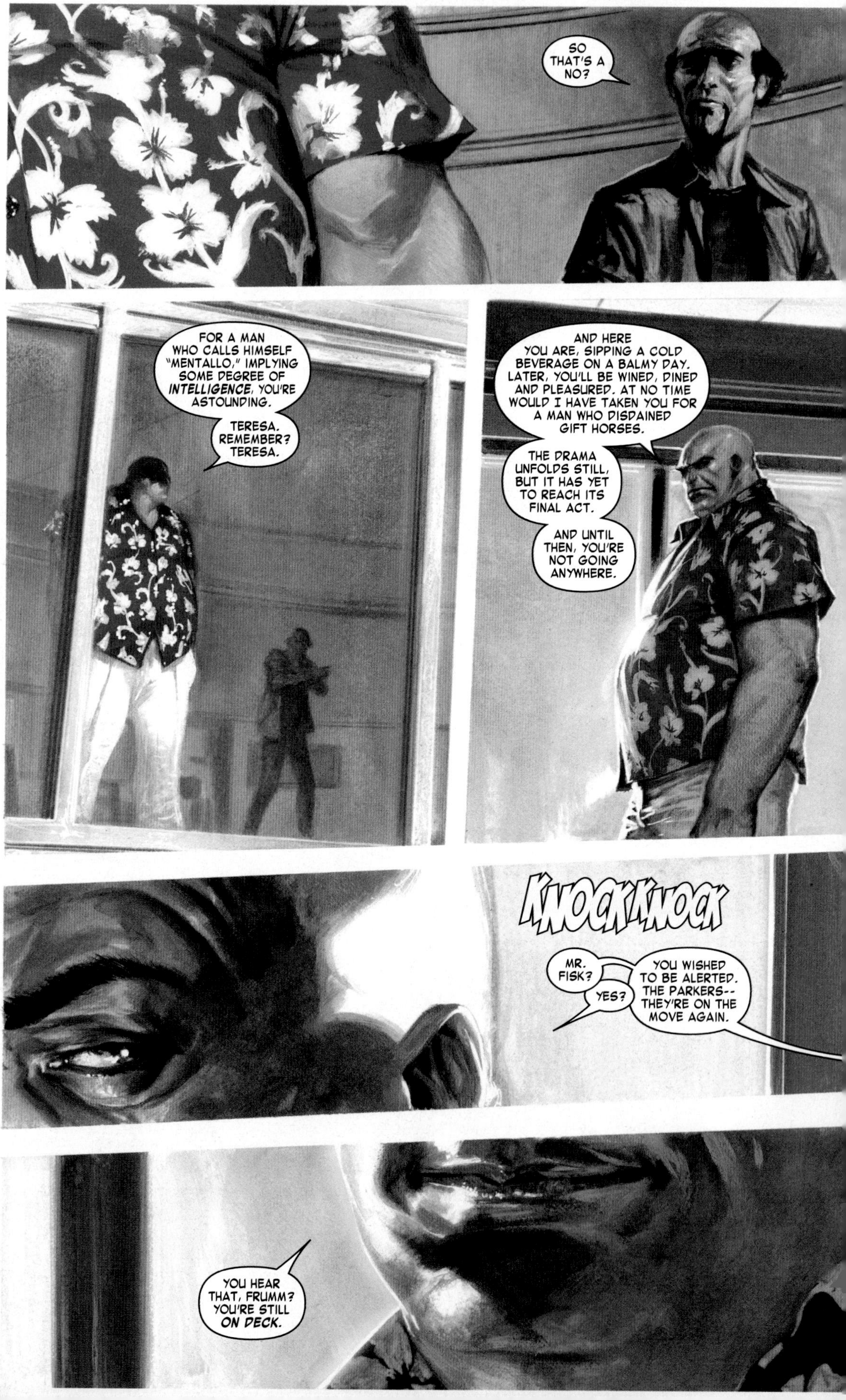
SO THAT'S A NO?
FOR A MAN WHO CALLS HIMSELF "MENTALLO," IMPLYING SOME DEGREE OF *INTELLIGENCE*, YOU'RE ASTOUNDING.
TERESA. REMEMBER? TERESA.
AND HERE YOU ARE, SIPPING A COLD BEVERAGE ON A BALMY DAY. LATER, YOU'LL BE WINED, DINED AND PLEASURED. AT NO TIME WOULD I HAVE TAKEN YOU FOR A MAN WHO DISDAINED GIFT HORSES.
THE DRAMA UNFOLDS STILL, BUT IT HAS YET TO REACH ITS FINAL ACT.
AND UNTIL THEN, YOU'RE NOT GOING ANYWHERE.
KNOCK KNOCK
MR. FISK?
YES?
YOU WISHED TO BE ALERTED. THE PARKERS--THEY'RE ON THE MOVE AGAIN.
YOU HEAR THAT, FRUMM? YOU'RE STILL *ON DECK*.

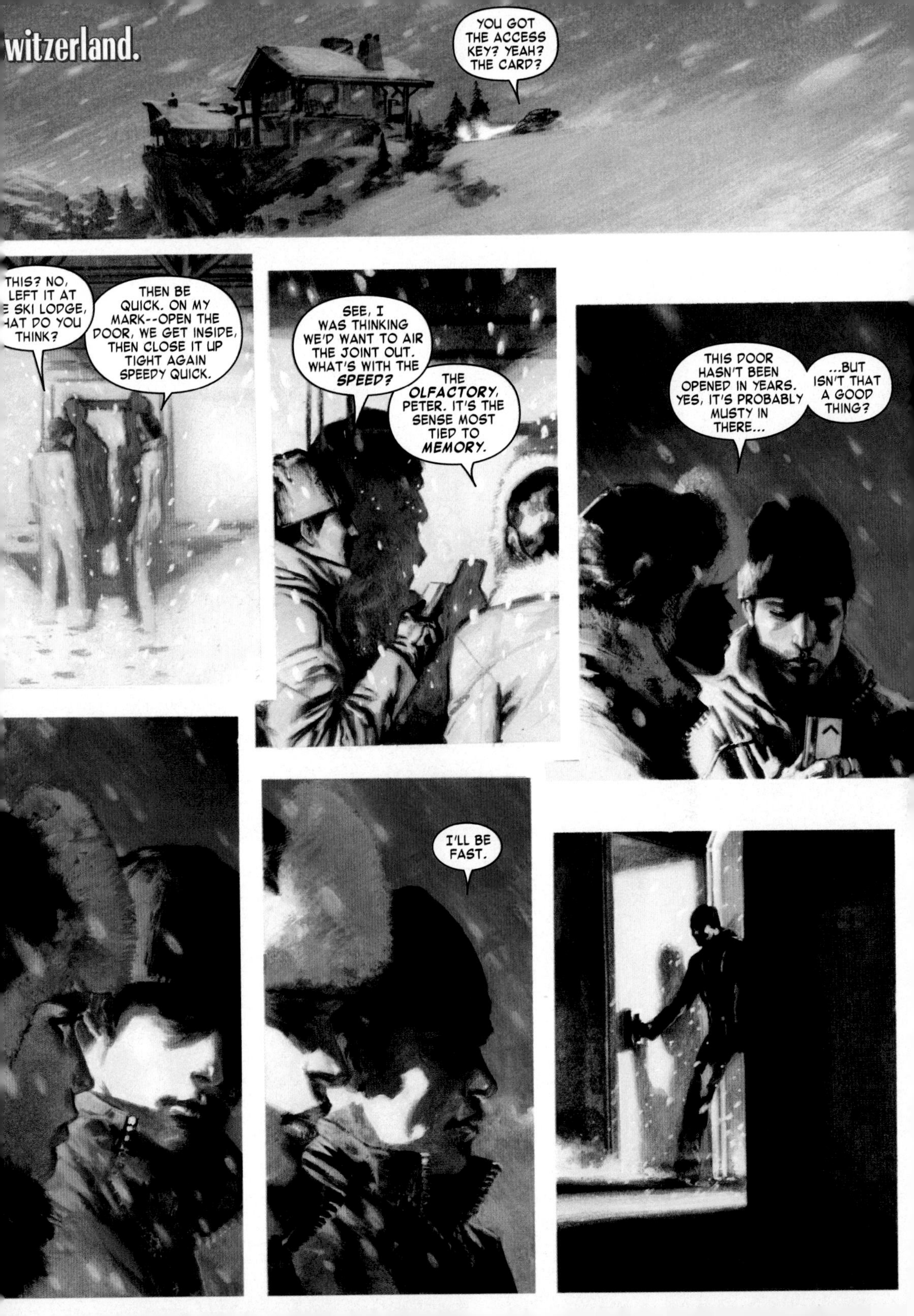
witzerland.
YOU GOT THE ACCESS KEY? YEAH? THE CARD?
THIS? NO, LEFT IT AT E SKI LODGE, HAT DO YOU THINK?
THEN BE QUICK. ON MY MARK--OPEN THE DOOR, WE GET INSIDE, THEN CLOSE IT UP TIGHT AGAIN SPEEDY QUICK.
SEE, I WAS THINKING WE'D WANT TO AIR THE JOINT OUT. WHAT'S WITH THE SPEED?
THE OLFACTORY, PETER. IT'S THE SENSE MOST TIED TO MEMORY.
THIS DOOR HASN'T BEEN OPENED IN YEARS. YES, IT'S PROBABLY MUSTY IN THERE...
...BUT ISN'T THAT A GOOD THING?
I'LL BE FAST.

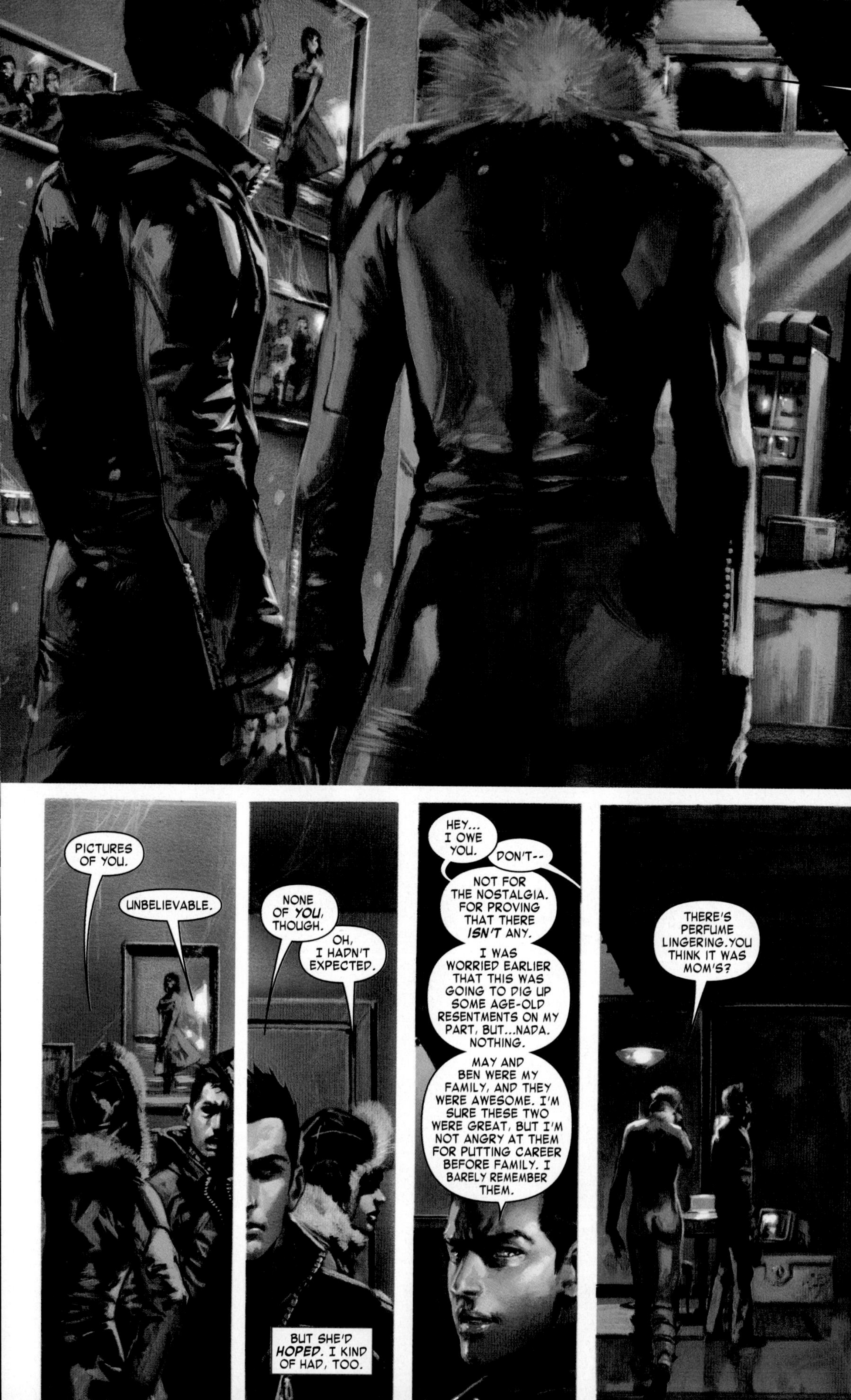

PICTURES OF YOU.
UNBELIEVABLE.
NONE OF *YOU*, THOUGH.
OH, I HADN'T EXPECTED.
BUT SHE'D *HOPED*. I KIND OF HAD, TOO.
HEY... I OWE YOU.
DON'T--
NOT FOR THE NOSTALGIA. FOR PROVING THAT THERE *ISN'T* ANY.
I WAS WORRIED EARLIER THAT THIS WAS GOING TO DIG UP SOME AGE-OLD RESENTMENTS ON MY PART, BUT...NADA. NOTHING.
MAY AND BEN WERE MY FAMILY, AND THEY WERE AWESOME. I'M SURE THESE TWO WERE GREAT, BUT I'M NOT ANGRY AT THEM FOR PUTTING CAREER BEFORE FAMILY. I BARELY REMEMBER THEM.
THERE'S PERFUME LINGERING. YOU THINK IT WAS MOM'S?

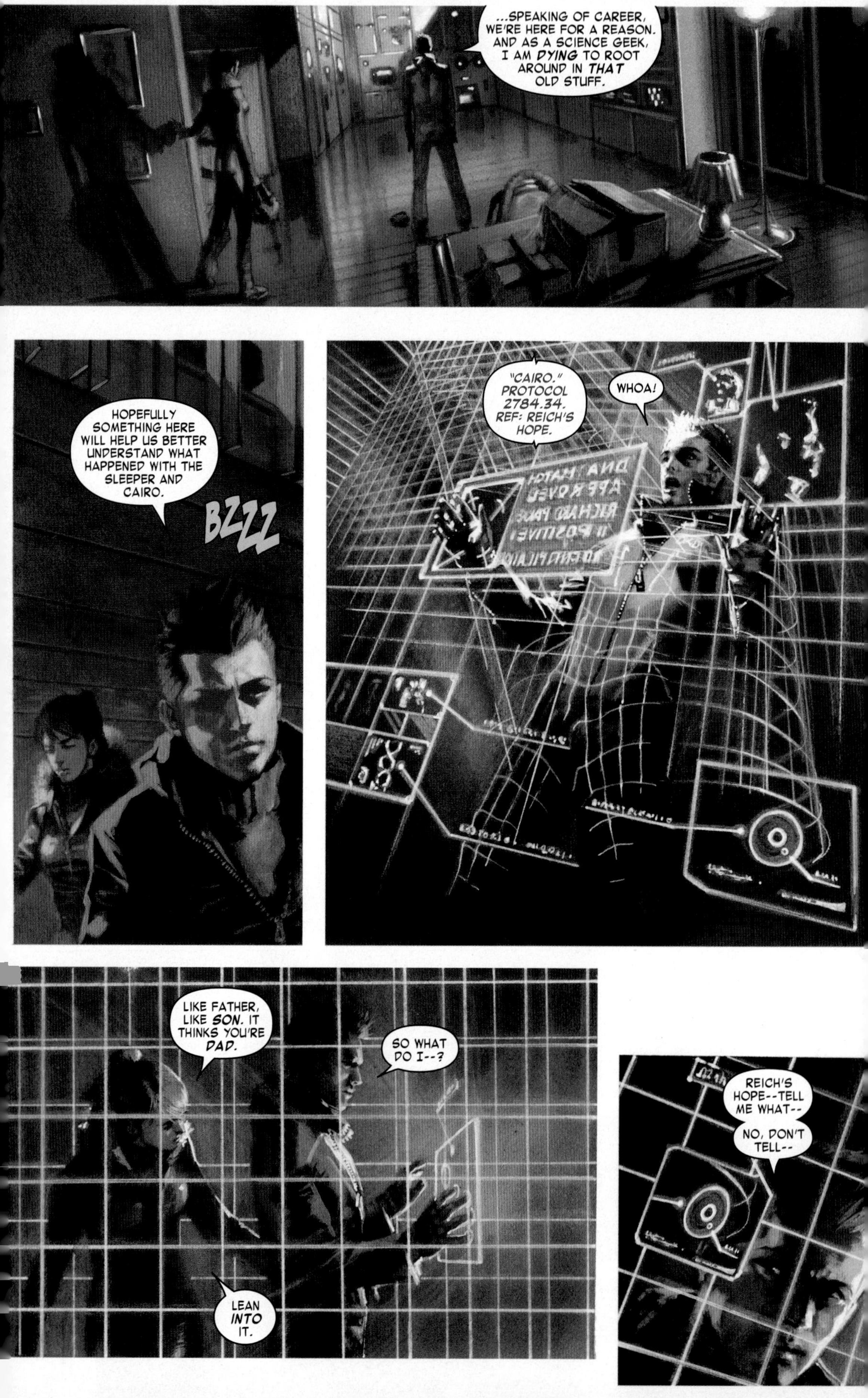
...SPEAKING OF CAREER, WE'RE HERE FOR A REASON. AND AS A SCIENCE GEEK, I AM DYING TO ROOT AROUND IN THAT OLD STUFF.
HOPEFULLY SOMETHING HERE WILL HELP US BETTER UNDERSTAND WHAT HAPPENED WITH THE SLEEPER AND CAIRO.
BZZZ
"CAIRO." PROTOCOL 2784.34. REF: REICH'S HOPE.
WHOA!
LIKE FATHER, LIKE SON. IT THINKS YOU'RE DAD.
SO WHAT DO I--?
LEAN INTO IT.
REICH'S HOPE--TELL ME WHAT--
NO, DON'T TELL--

RELAX. WE CAN SPARE A MINUTE OR--

WRONG AGAIN.

SPIDER-SENSES, GOING CRAZY. ZERO TO *LIGHT SPEED* IN NO TIME.

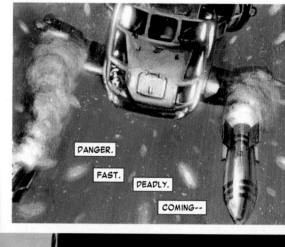

DANGER.

FAST.

DEADLY.

COMING--

TERESA!

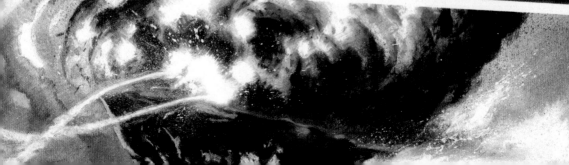

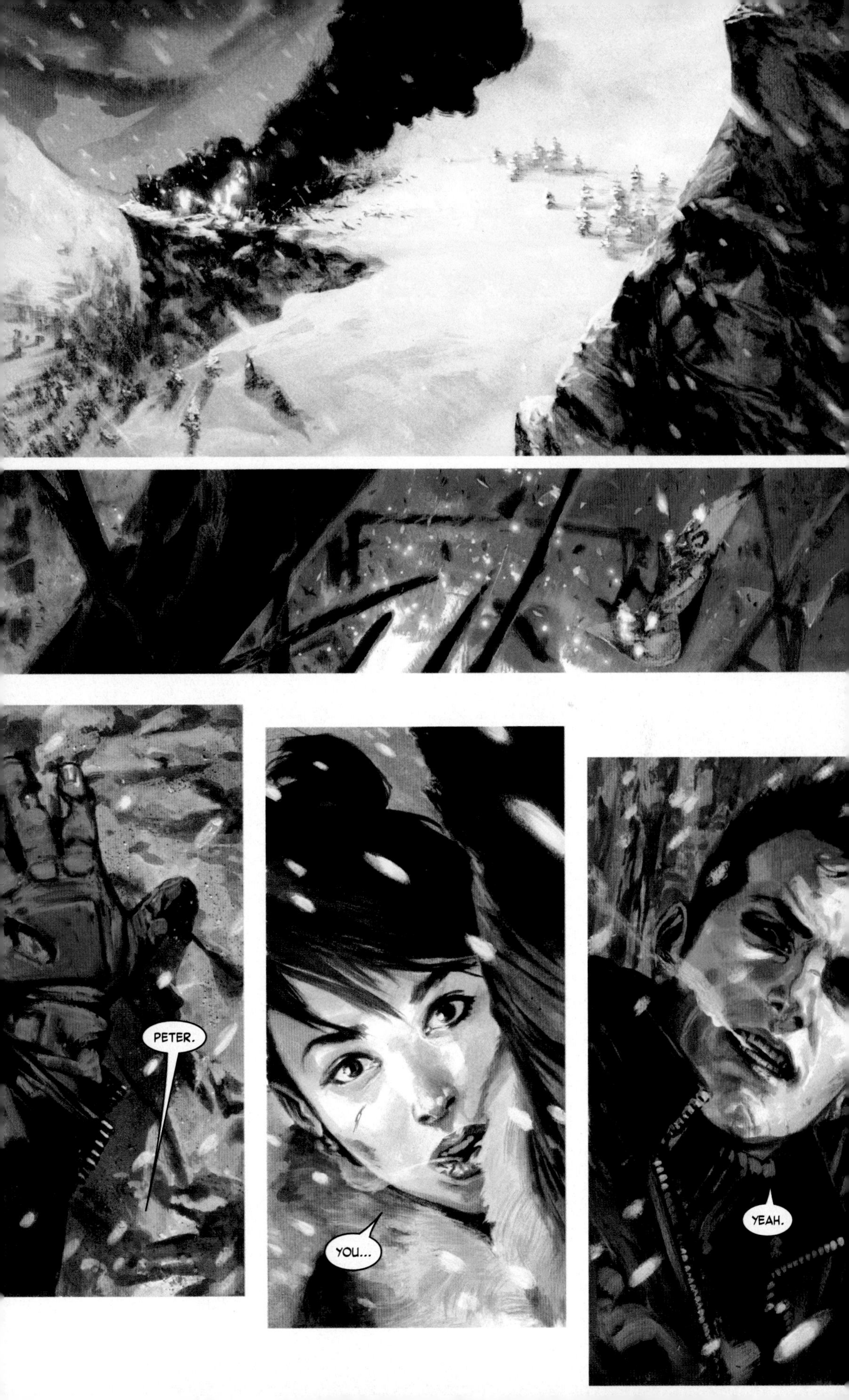
PETER.
YOU...
YEAH.

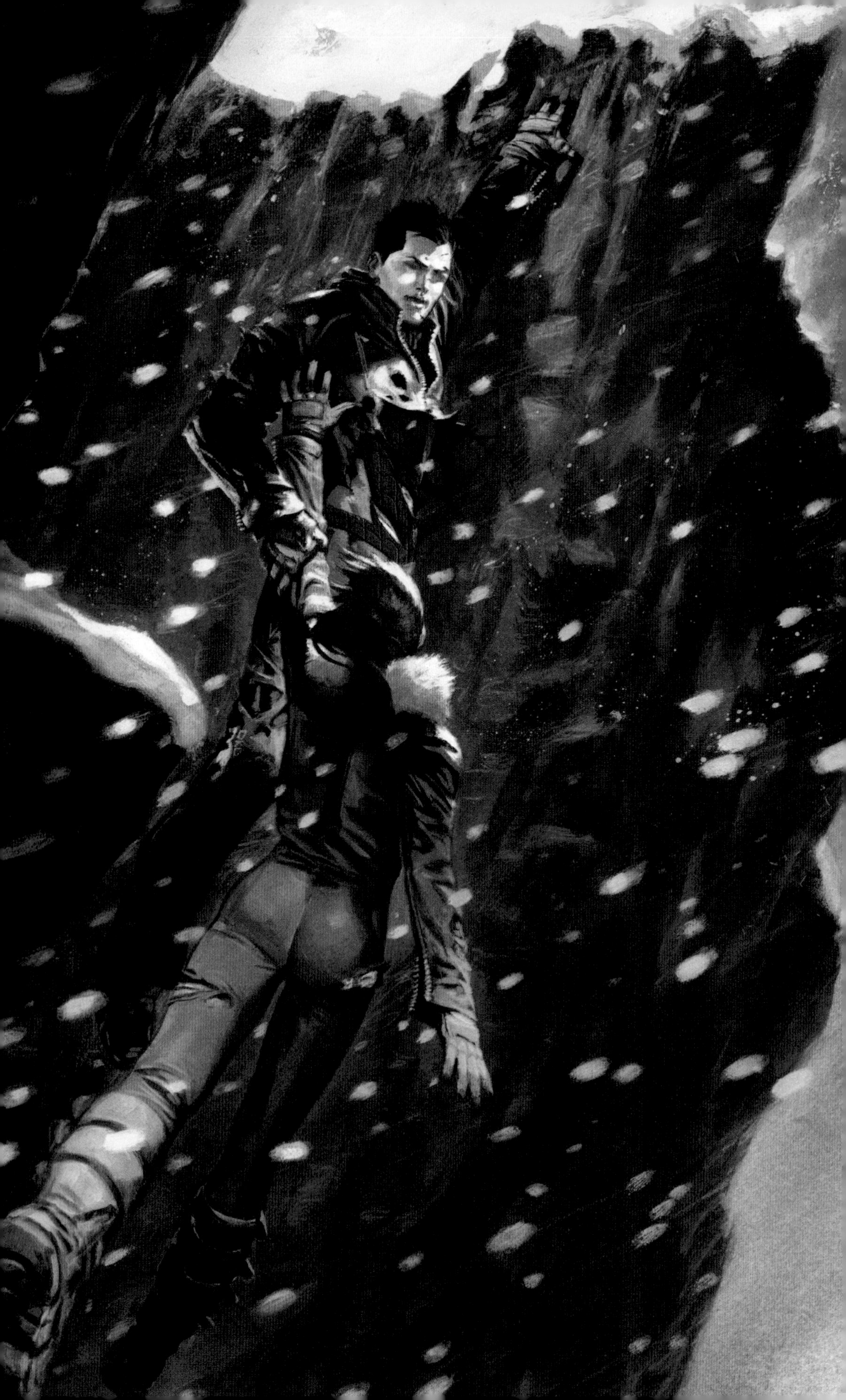

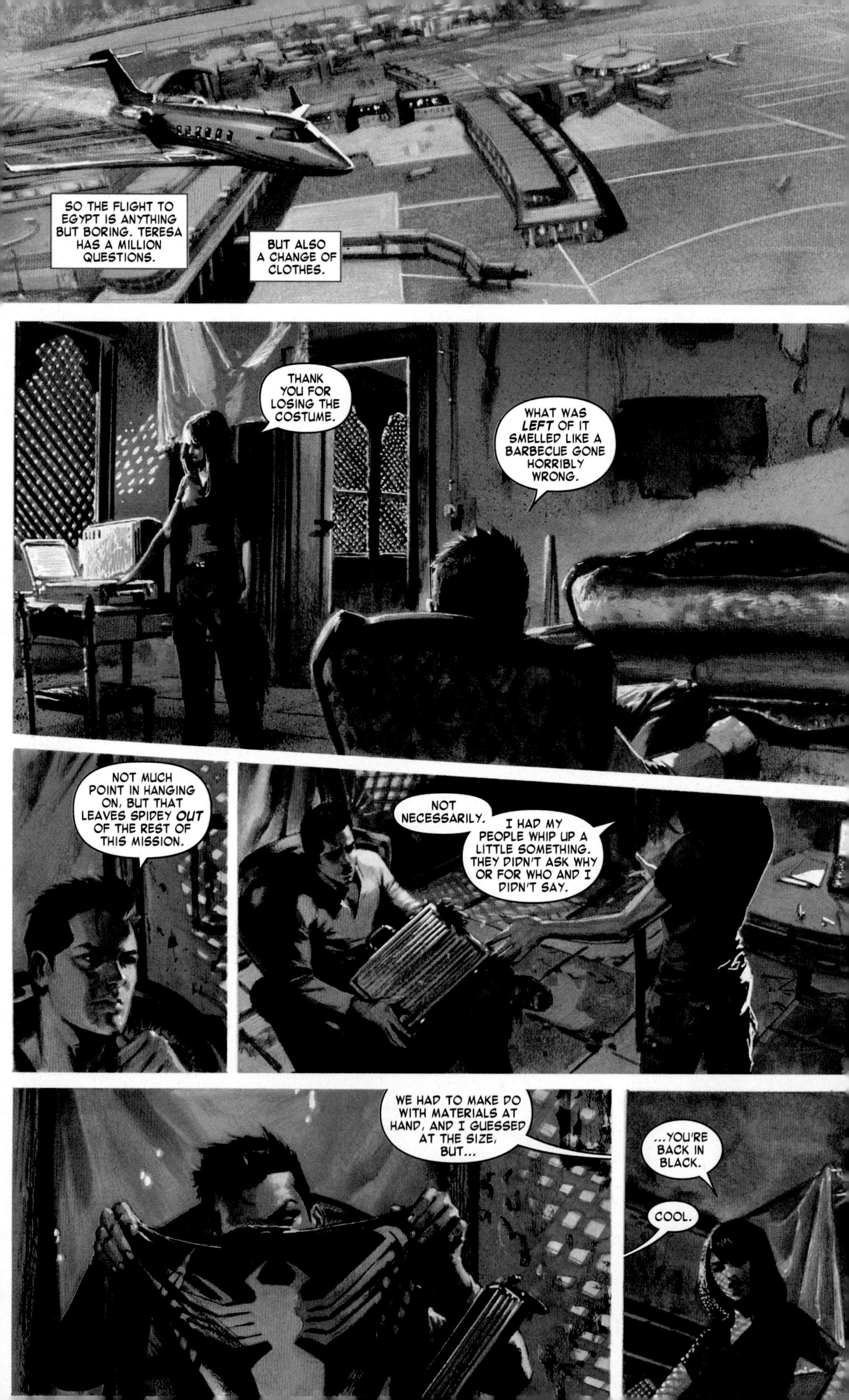
SO THE FLIGHT TO EGYPT IS ANYTHING BUT BORING. TERESA HAS A MILLION QUESTIONS.
BUT ALSO A CHANGE OF CLOTHES.
THANK YOU FOR LOSING THE COSTUME.
WHAT WAS *LEFT* OF IT SMELLED LIKE A BARBECUE GONE HORRIBLY WRONG.
NOT MUCH POINT IN HANGING ON, BUT THAT LEAVES SPIDEY *OUT* OF THE REST OF THIS MISSION.
NOT NECESSARILY.
I HAD MY PEOPLE WHIP UP A LITTLE SOMETHING. THEY DIDN'T ASK WHY OR FOR WHO AND I DIDN'T SAY.
WE HAD TO MAKE DO WITH MATERIALS AT HAND, AND I GUESSED AT THE SIZE, BUT...
...YOU'RE BACK IN BLACK.
COOL.

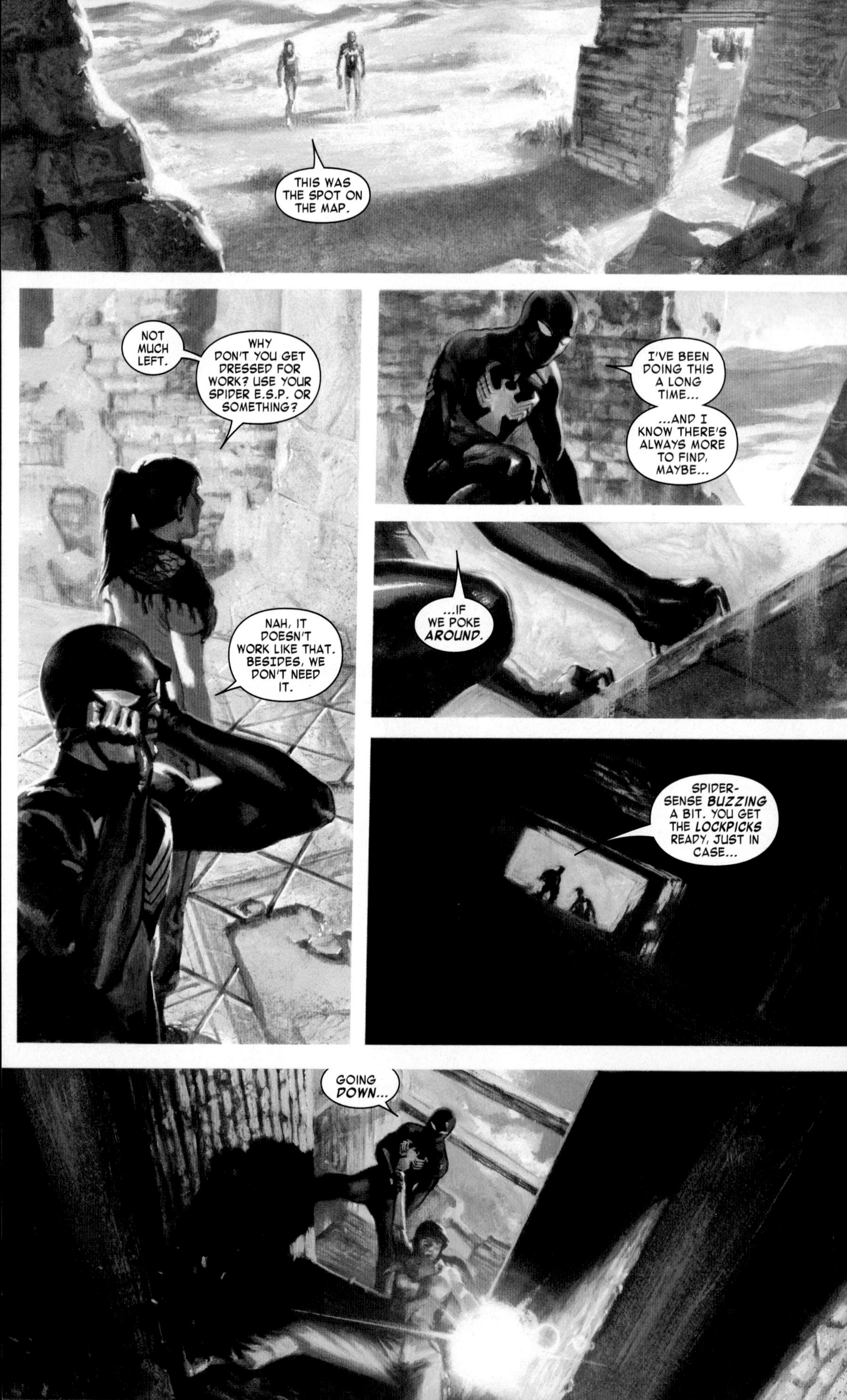
THIS WAS THE SPOT ON THE MAP.
NOT MUCH LEFT.
WHY DON'T YOU GET DRESSED FOR WORK? USE YOUR SPIDER E.S.P. OR SOMETHING?
NAH, IT DOESN'T WORK LIKE THAT. BESIDES, WE DON'T NEED IT.
I'VE BEEN DOING THIS A LONG TIME...
...AND I KNOW THERE'S ALWAYS MORE TO FIND, MAYBE...
...IF WE POKE AROUND.
SPIDER-SENSE BUZZING A BIT. YOU GET THE LOCKPICKS READY, JUST IN CASE...
GOING DOWN...

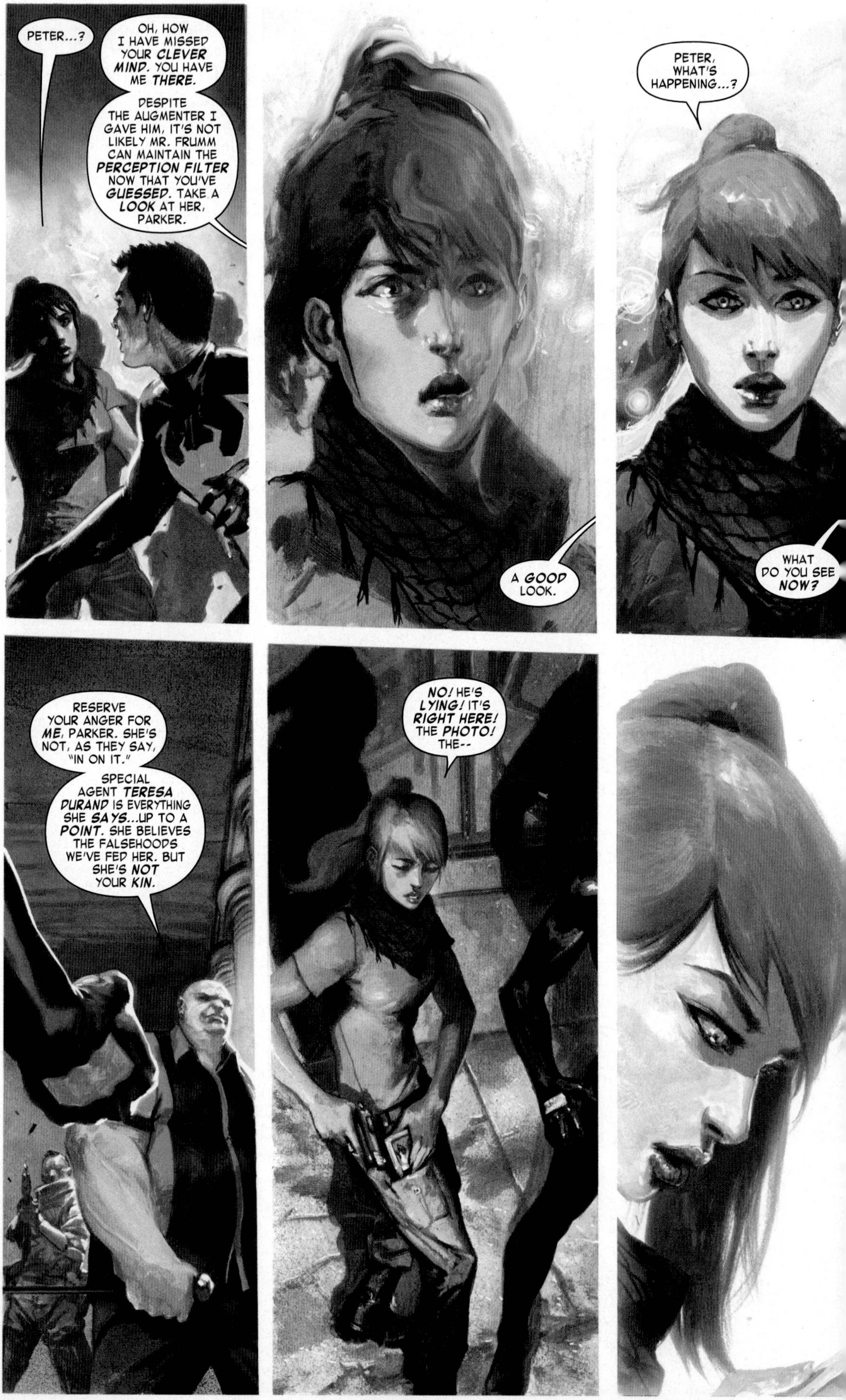
PETER...?
OH, HOW I HAVE MISSED YOUR CLEVER MIND. YOU HAVE ME THERE.
DESPITE THE AUGMENTER I GAVE HIM, IT'S NOT LIKELY MR. FRUMM CAN MAINTAIN THE PERCEPTION FILTER NOW THAT YOU'VE GUESSED. TAKE A LOOK AT HER, PARKER.
A GOOD LOOK.
PETER, WHAT'S HAPPENING...?
WHAT DO YOU SEE NOW?
RESERVE YOUR ANGER FOR ME, PARKER. SHE'S NOT, AS THEY SAY, "IN ON IT."
SPECIAL AGENT TERESA DURAND IS EVERYTHING SHE SAYS...UP TO A POINT. SHE BELIEVES THE FALSEHOODS WE'VE FED HER. BUT SHE'S NOT YOUR KIN.
NO! HE'S LYING! IT'S RIGHT HERE! THE PHOTO! THE--

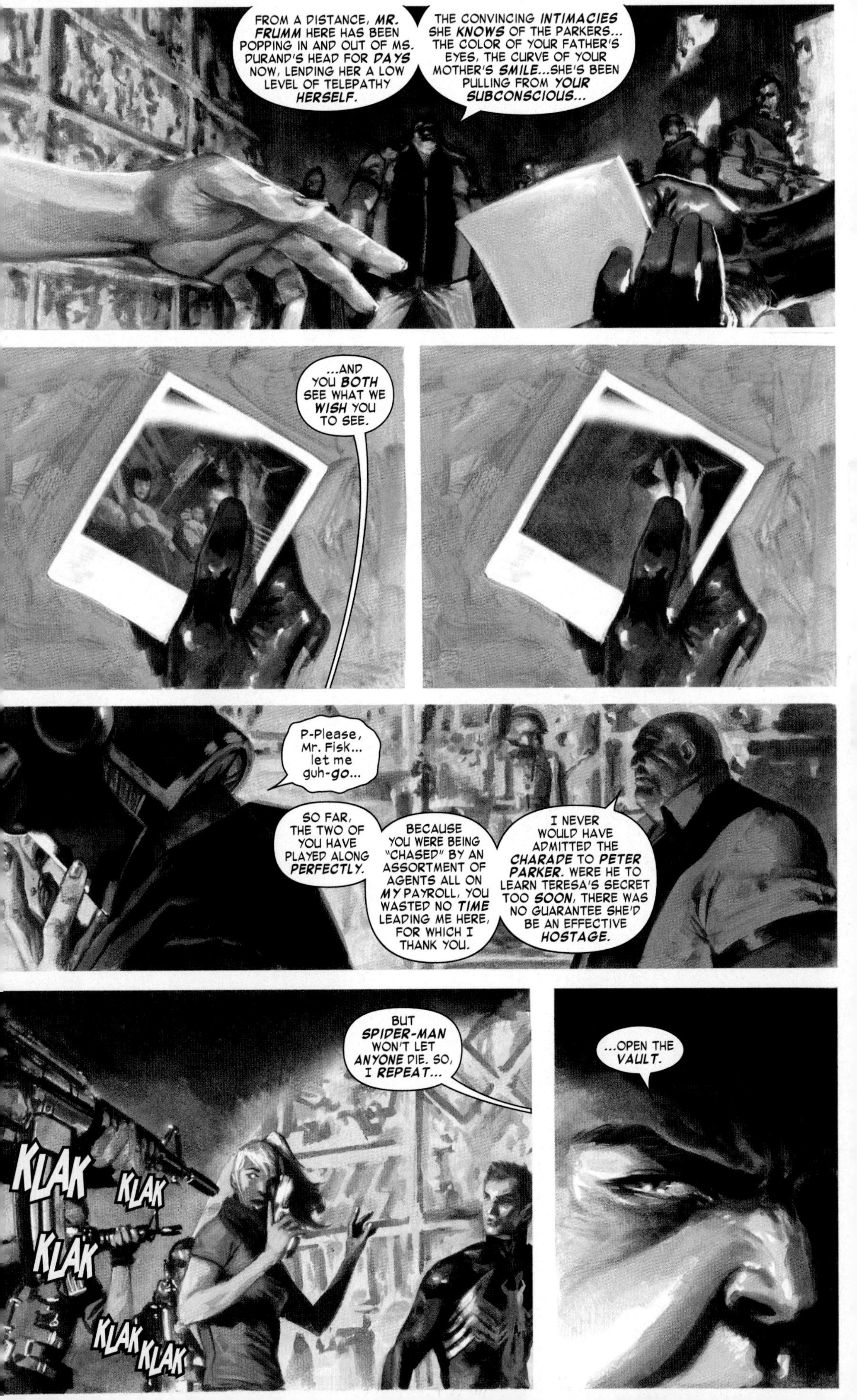
FROM A DISTANCE, MR. FRUMM HERE HAS BEEN POPPING IN AND OUT OF MS. DURAND'S HEAD FOR DAYS NOW, LENDING HER A LOW LEVEL OF TELEPATHY HERSELF.
THE CONVINCING INTIMACIES SHE KNOWS OF THE PARKERS... THE COLOR OF YOUR FATHER'S EYES, THE CURVE OF YOUR MOTHER'S SMILE...SHE'S BEEN PULLING FROM YOUR SUBCONSCIOUS...
...AND YOU BOTH SEE WHAT WE WISH YOU TO SEE.
P-Please, Mr. Fisk... let me guh-go...
SO FAR, THE TWO OF YOU HAVE PLAYED ALONG PERFECTLY.
BECAUSE YOU WERE BEING "CHASED" BY AN ASSORTMENT OF AGENTS ALL ON MY PAYROLL, YOU WASTED NO TIME LEADING ME HERE, FOR WHICH I THANK YOU.
I NEVER WOULD HAVE ADMITTED THE CHARADE TO PETER PARKER. WERE HE TO LEARN TERESA'S SECRET TOO SOON, THERE WAS NO GUARANTEE SHE'D BE AN EFFECTIVE HOSTAGE.
BUT SPIDER-MAN WON'T LET ANYONE DIE. SO, I REPEAT...
KLAK
KLAK
KLAK
KLAK KLAK
...OPEN THE VAULT.

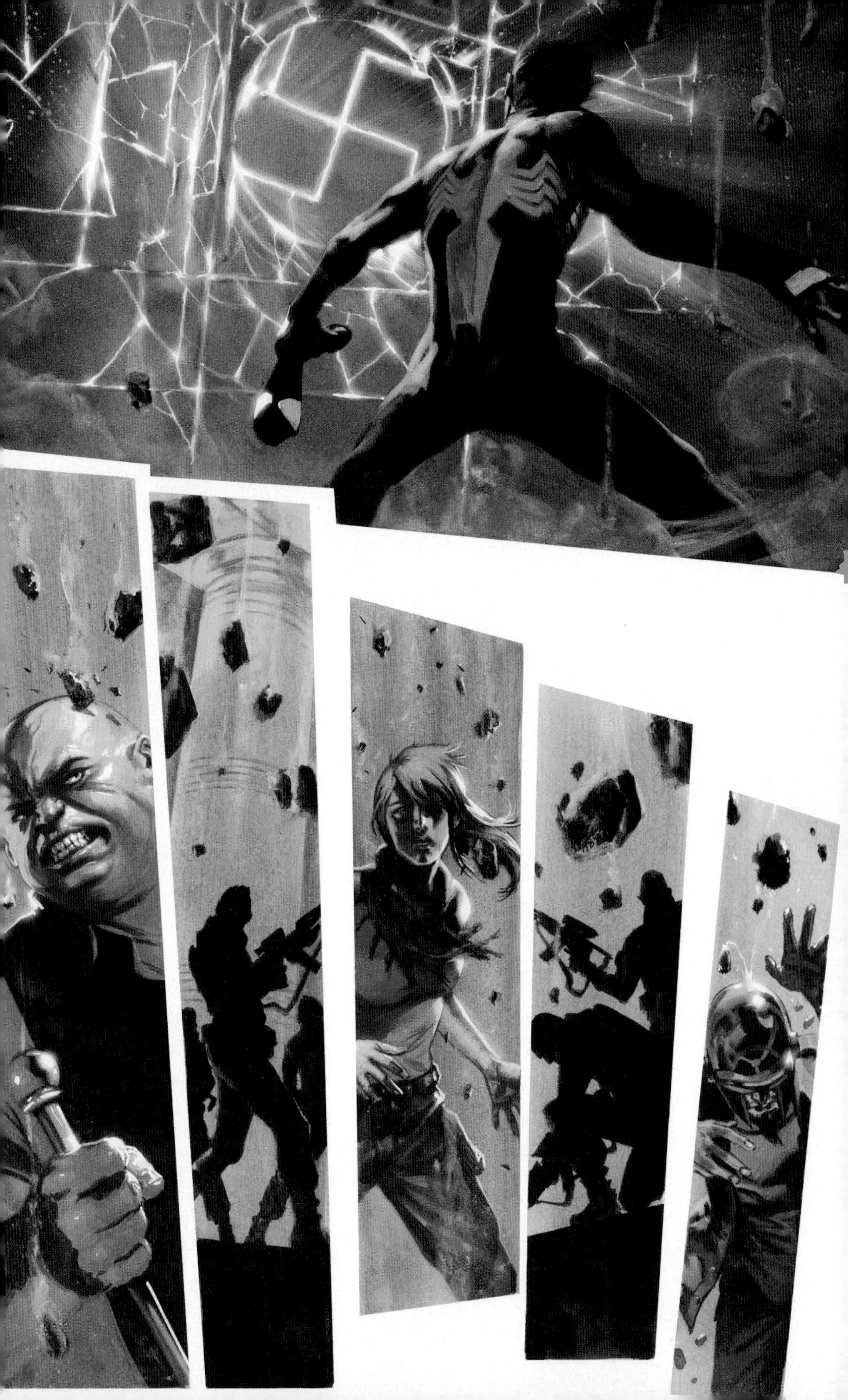

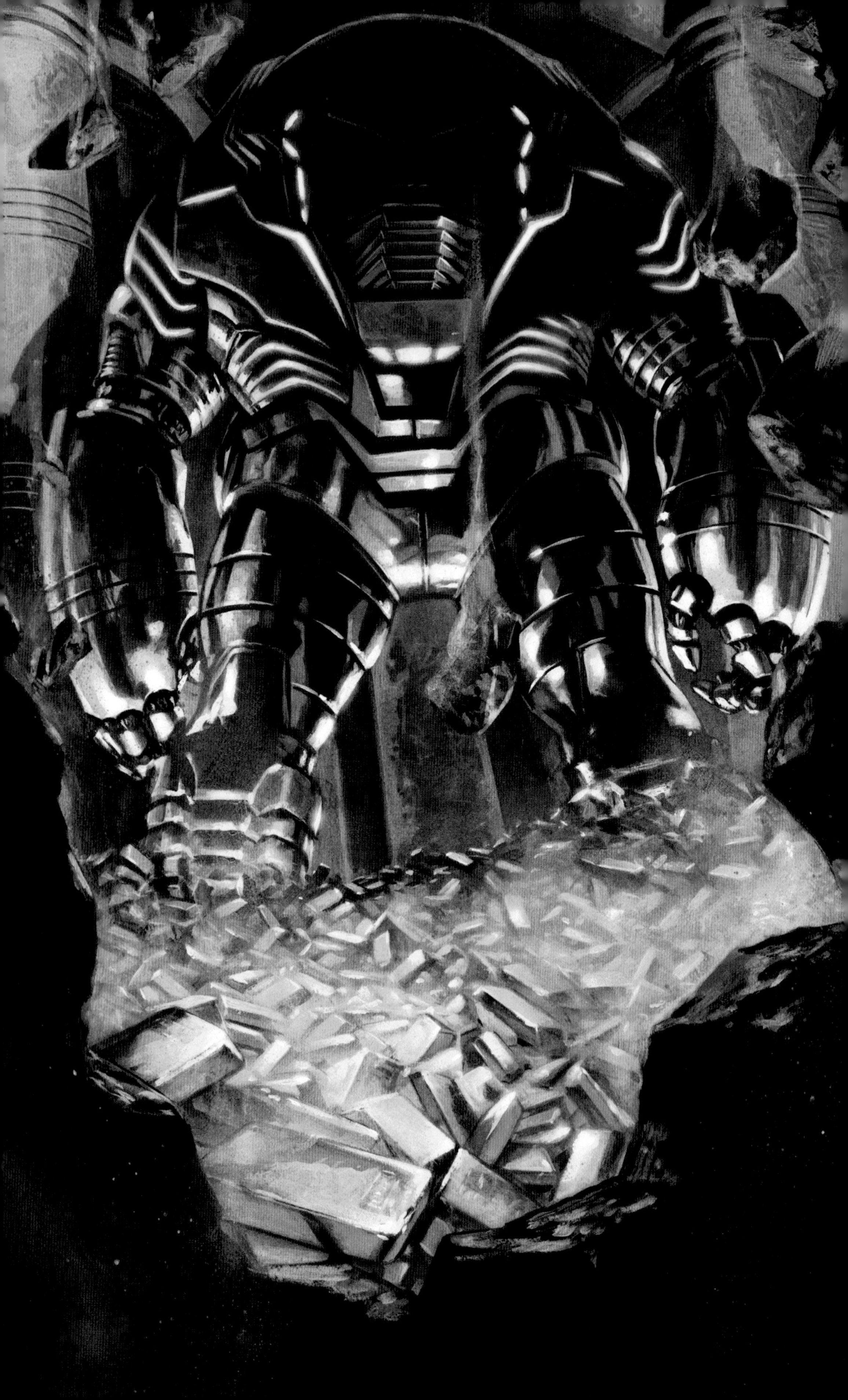

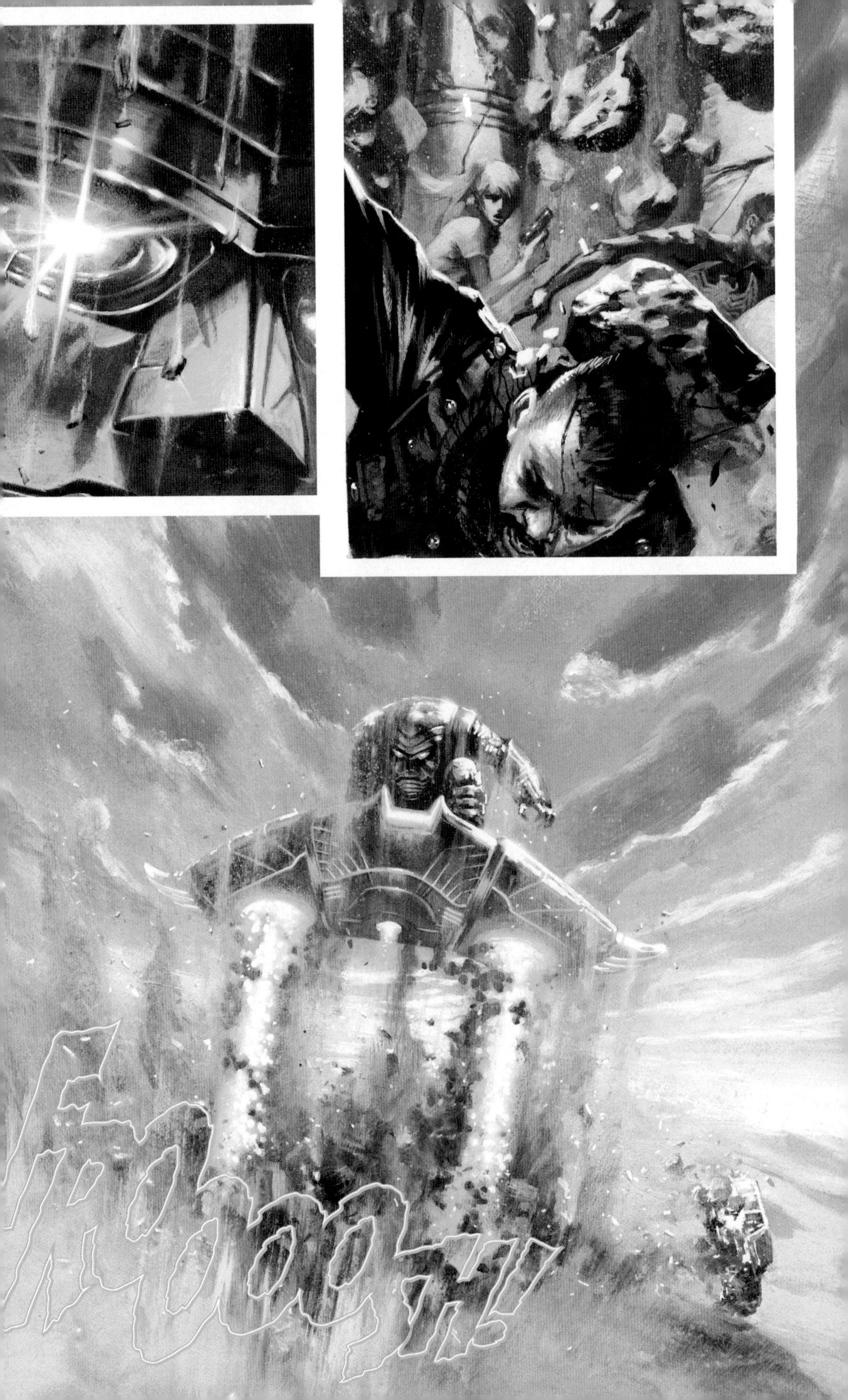
Fhooom!

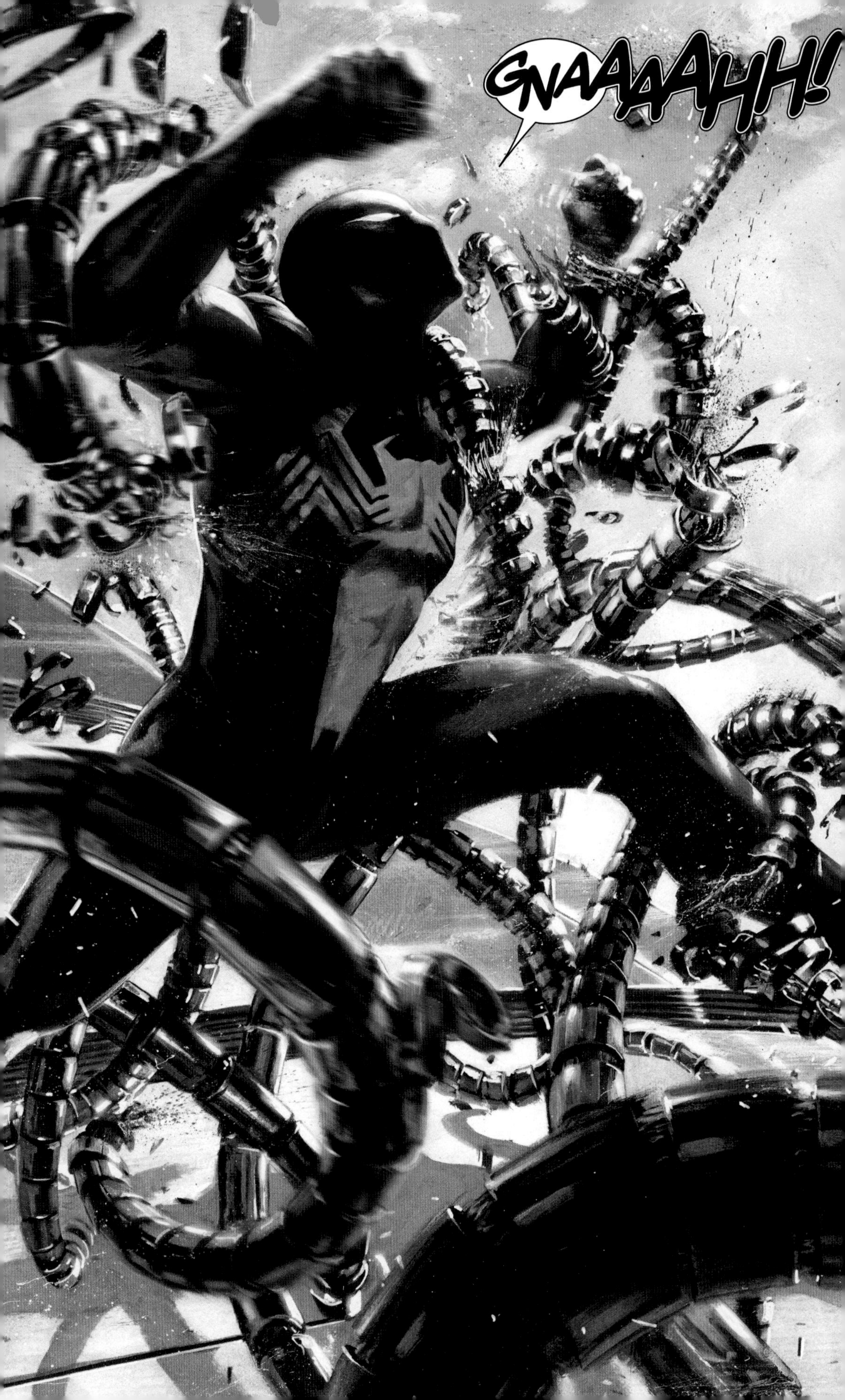
GNAAAAAHH!

RATATATATATAT
TATATAT

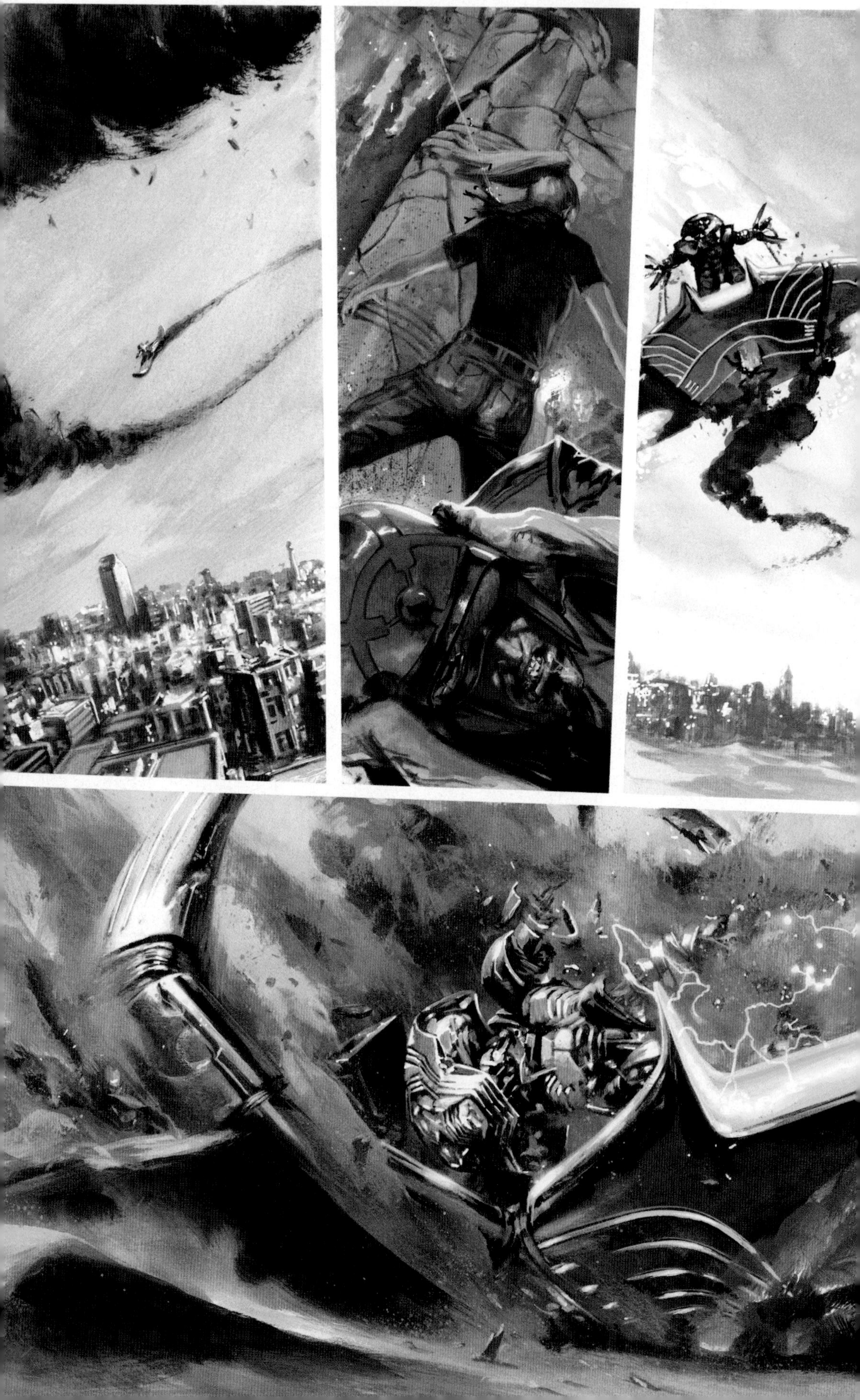

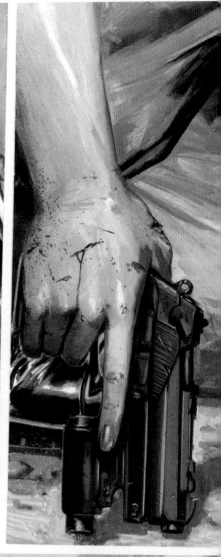
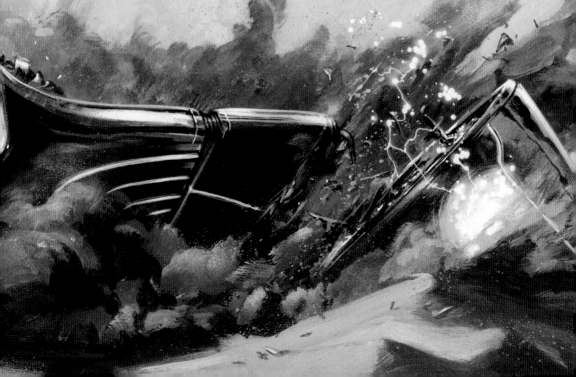

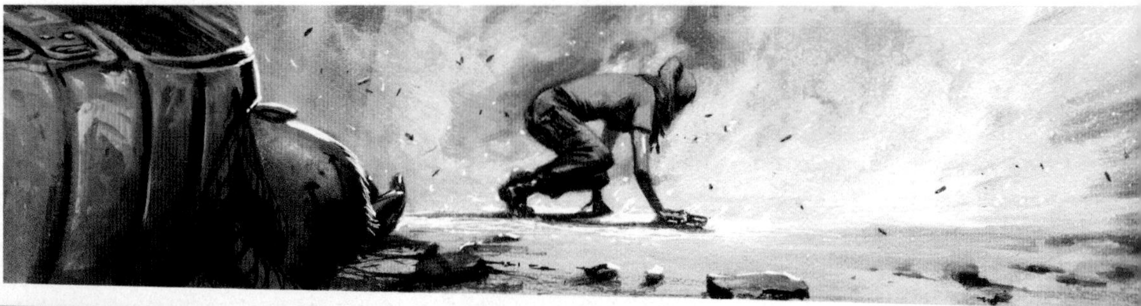

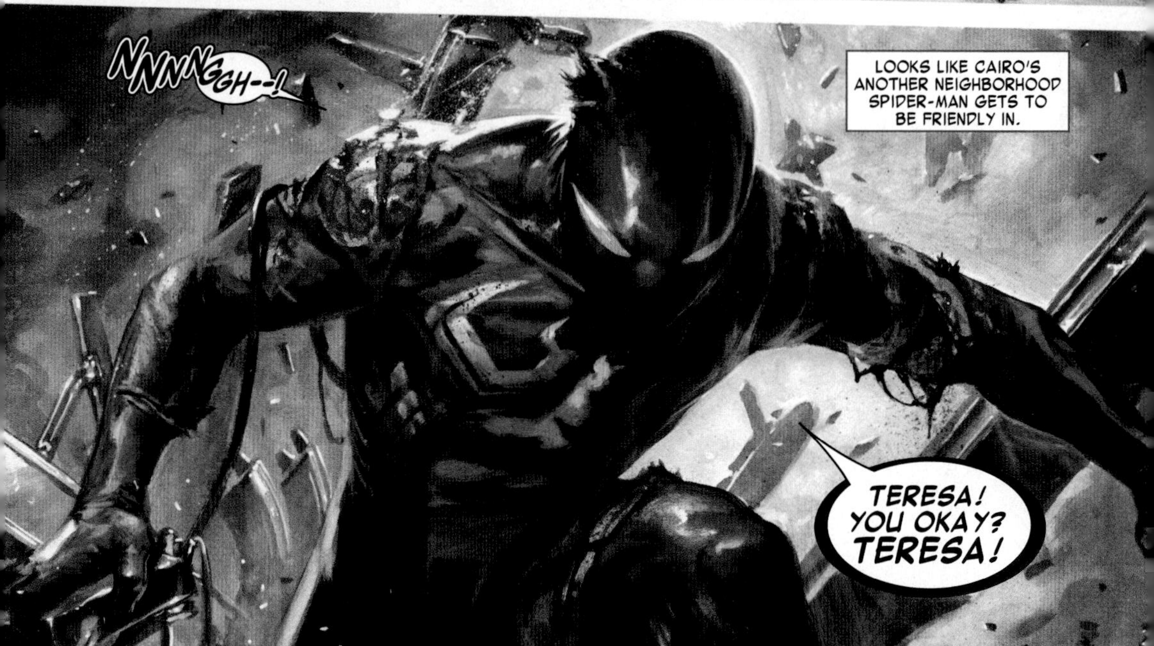
NNNNGGH--!
LOOKS LIKE CAIRO'S ANOTHER NEIGHBORHOOD SPIDER-MAN GETS TO BE FRIENDLY IN.
TERESA! YOU OKAY? TERESA!

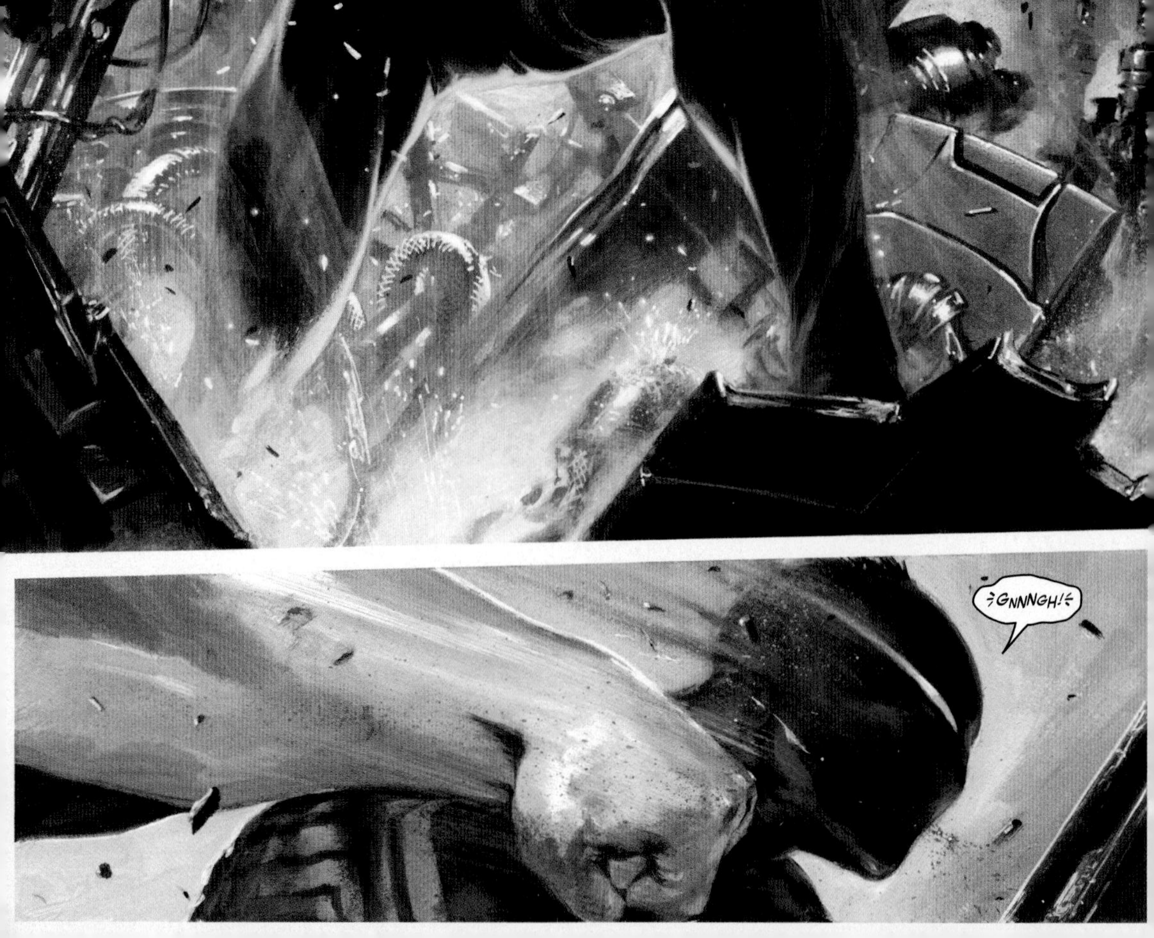
GNNNGH!

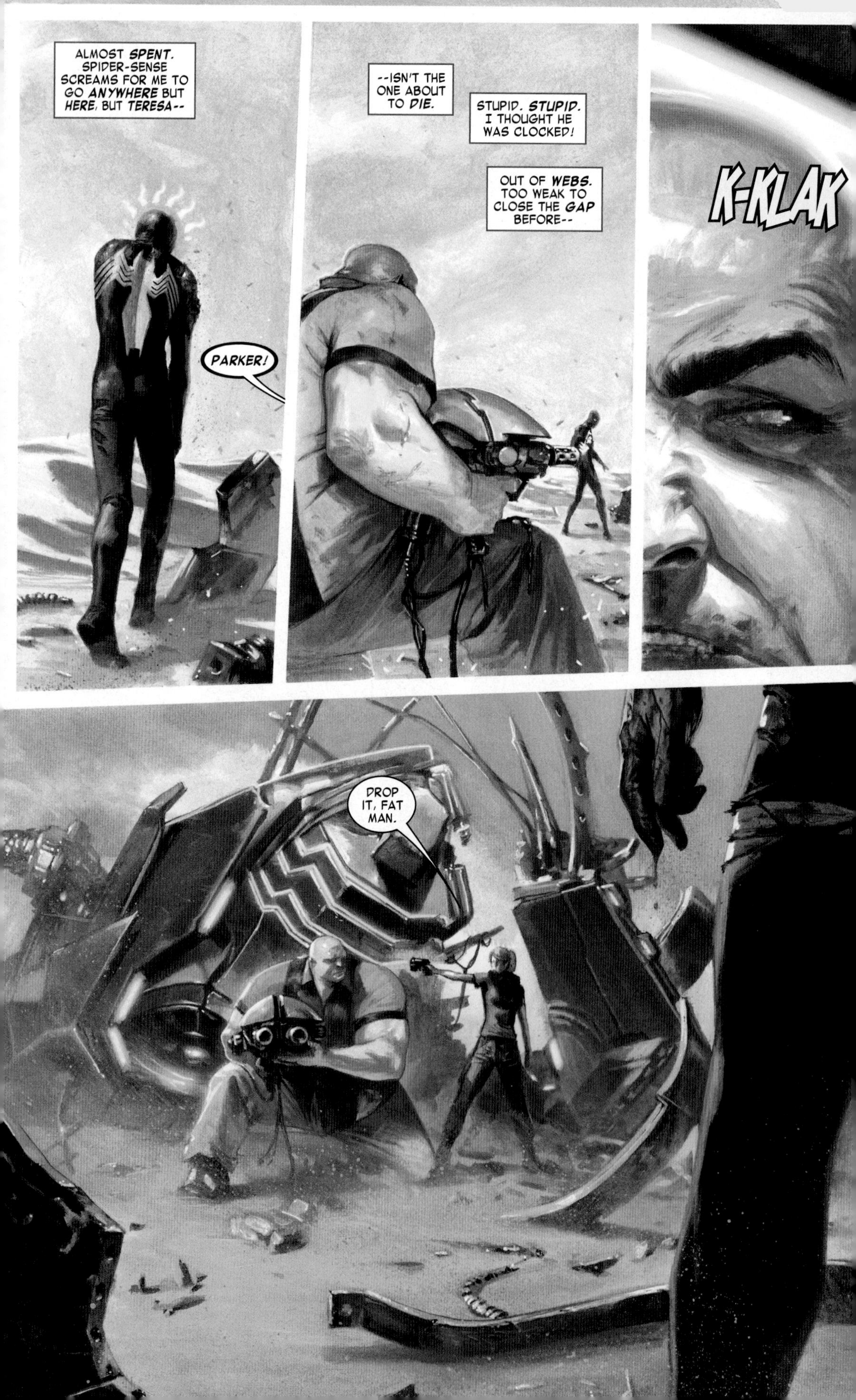
ALMOST *SPENT.* SPIDER-SENSE SCREAMS FOR ME TO GO *ANYWHERE* BUT *HERE,* BUT *TERESA*--
PARKER!
--ISN'T THE ONE ABOUT TO *DIE.*
STUPID. *STUPID.* I THOUGHT HE WAS CLOCKED!
OUT OF *WEBS.* TOO WEAK TO CLOSE THE *GAP* BEFORE--
K-KLAK
DROP IT, FAT MAN.

YOU ARE AS FAR AS *I'M* CONCERNED.

BLAM

GHAAAH!

I OFFERED TO LET YOU *SERVE* ME. YOU SHOULD HAVE *ACCEPTED.*

ƷHKK-KK-Kϵ

...NO...

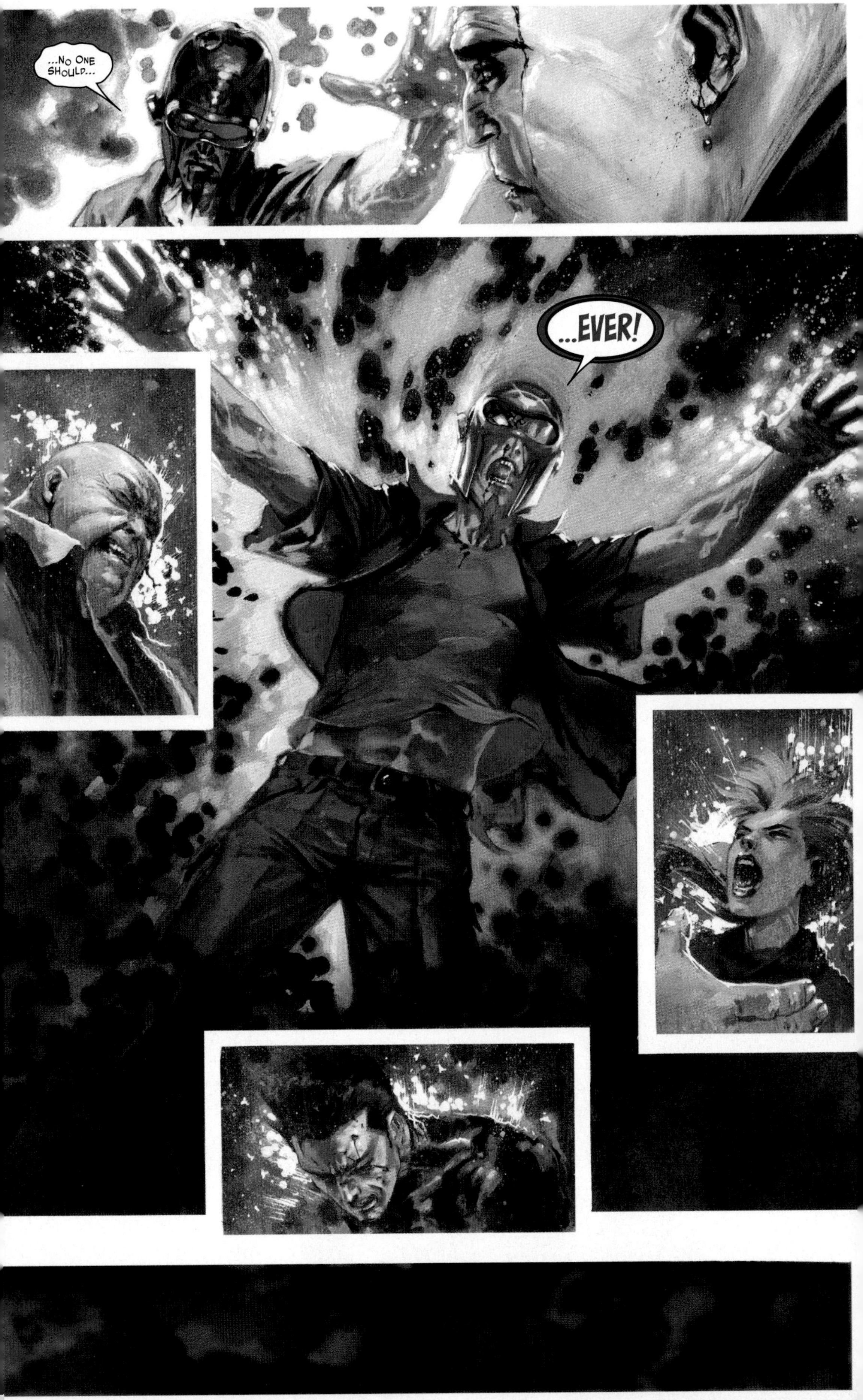
...NO ONE SHOULD...
...EVER!

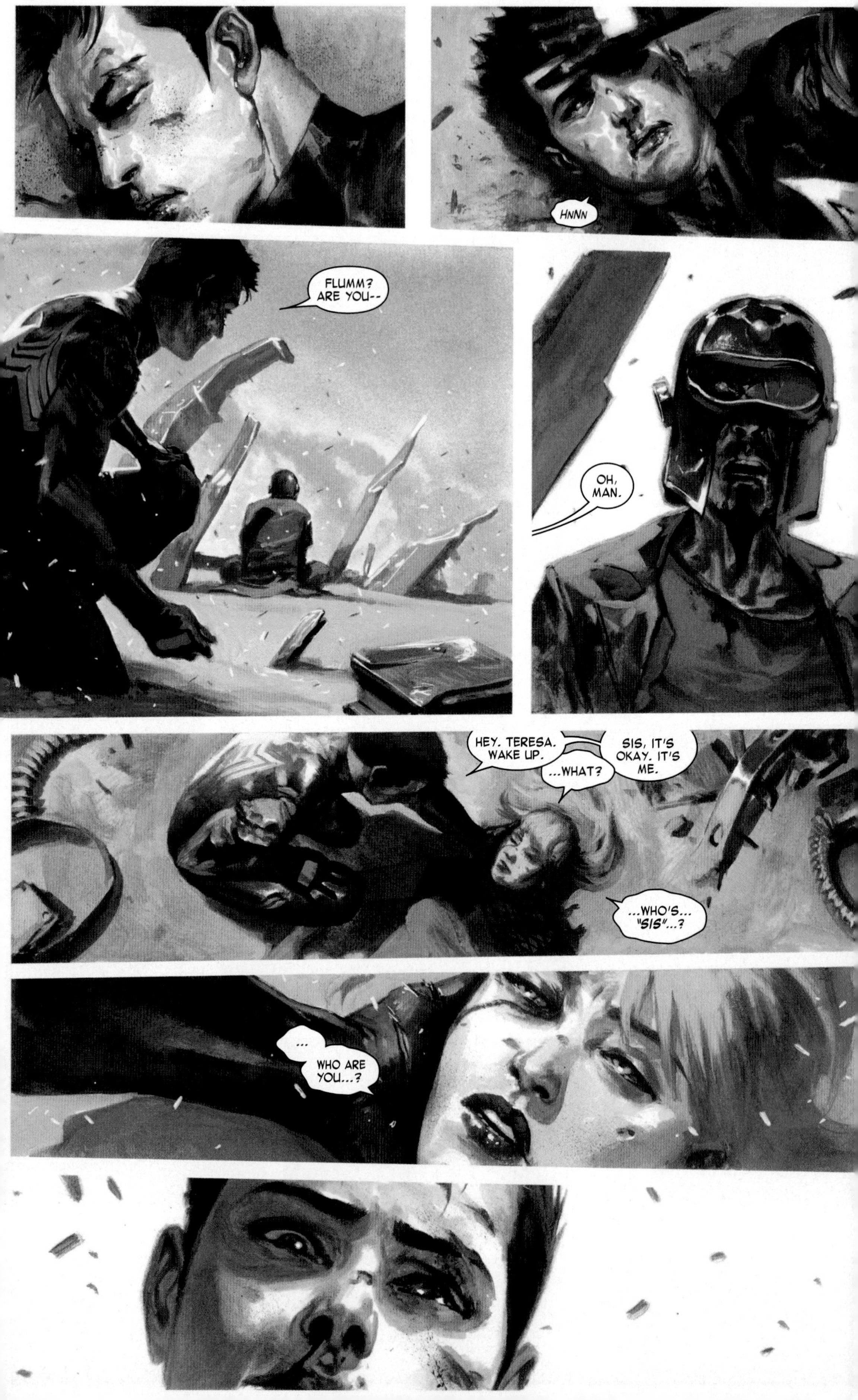
HNNN
FLUMM? ARE YOU--
OH, MAN.
HEY. TERESA. WAKE UP.
...WHAT?
SIS, IT'S OKAY. IT'S ME.
...WHO'S... "SIS"...?
... WHO ARE YOU...?

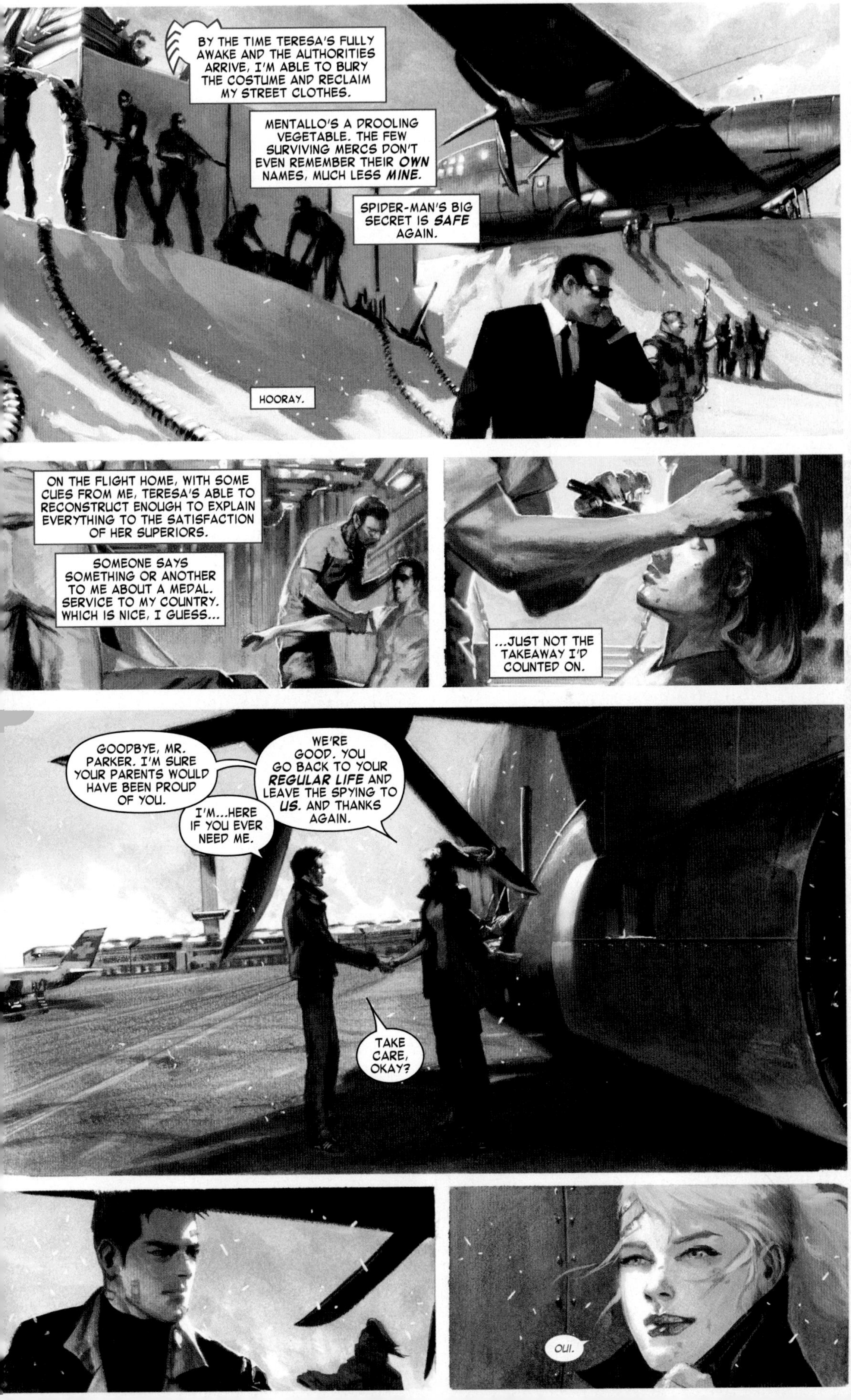
BY THE TIME TERESA'S FULLY AWAKE AND THE AUTHORITIES ARRIVE, I'M ABLE TO BURY THE COSTUME AND RECLAIM MY STREET CLOTHES.
MENTALLO'S A DROOLING VEGETABLE. THE FEW SURVIVING MERCS DON'T EVEN REMEMBER THEIR OWN NAMES, MUCH LESS MINE.
SPIDER-MAN'S BIG SECRET IS SAFE AGAIN.
HOORAY.
ON THE FLIGHT HOME, WITH SOME CUES FROM ME, TERESA'S ABLE TO RECONSTRUCT ENOUGH TO EXPLAIN EVERYTHING TO THE SATISFACTION OF HER SUPERIORS.
SOMEONE SAYS SOMETHING OR ANOTHER TO ME ABOUT A MEDAL. SERVICE TO MY COUNTRY. WHICH IS NICE, I GUESS...
...JUST NOT THE TAKEAWAY I'D COUNTED ON.
GOODBYE, MR. PARKER. I'M SURE YOUR PARENTS WOULD HAVE BEEN PROUD OF YOU.
WE'RE GOOD. YOU GO BACK TO YOUR REGULAR LIFE AND LEAVE THE SPYING TO US. AND THANKS AGAIN.
I'M...HERE IF YOU EVER NEED ME.
TAKE CARE, OKAY?
OUI.

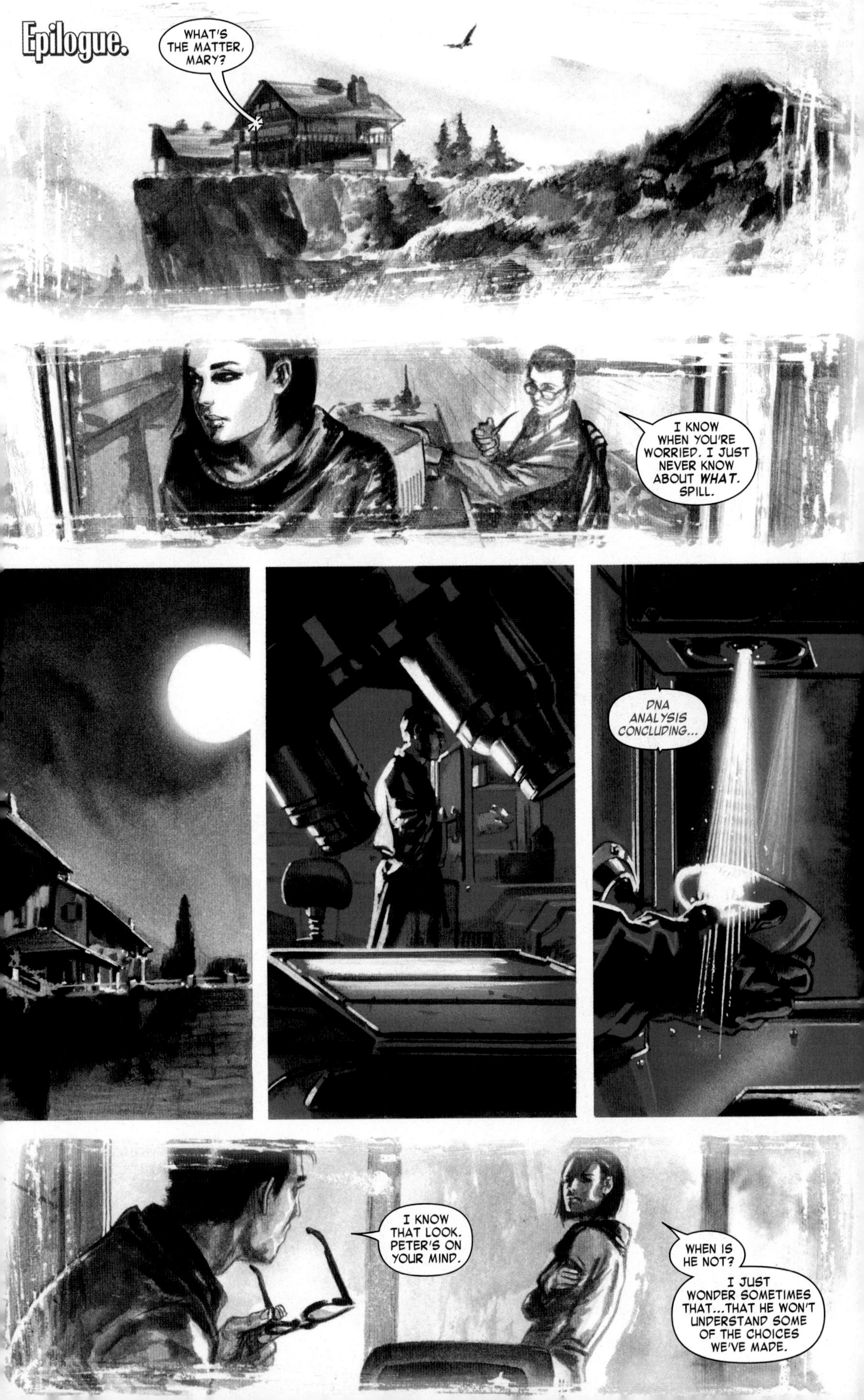

Epilogue.
WHAT'S THE MATTER, MARY?
I KNOW WHEN YOU'RE WORRIED. I JUST NEVER KNOW ABOUT WHAT. SPILL.
DNA ANALYSIS CONCLUDING...
I KNOW THAT LOOK. PETER'S ON YOUR MIND.
WHEN IS HE NOT?
I JUST WONDER SOMETIMES THAT...THAT HE WON'T UNDERSTAND SOME OF THE CHOICES WE'VE MADE.

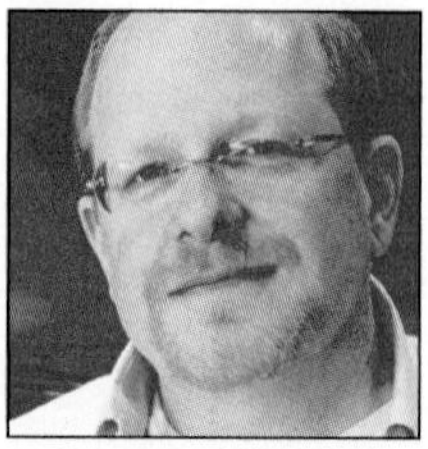

New York Times best-selling author **Mark Waid** has worked for every major company in the comics industry in a nearly three-decade career, writing thousands of issues including runs of *Amazing Spider-Man*, *X-Men*, *Ka-Zar* and *Fantastic Four.* His other works of note include his collaboration with painter Alex Ross, *Kingdom Come,* which earned an Eisner Award for Best Limited Series, and his long run on DC's *Flash.* He is enjoying great critical acclaim with the Eisner Award-winning *Daredevil.*

Biographies

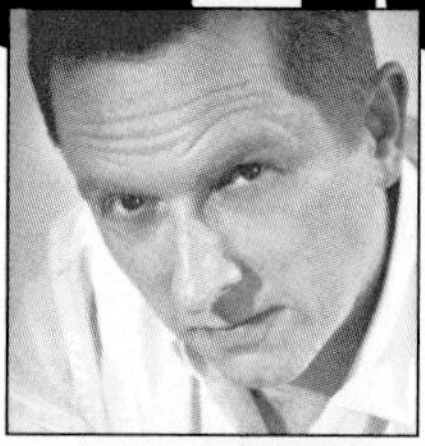

British writer **James Robinson** is acclaimed for his runs on DC's *Starman*, *Justice Society of America* and *Superman*. For Marvel, he has scripted *Generation X*, *Fantastic Four* and *All-New Invaders*. He has written several feature-film screenplays – including the adaptation of the comic book *The League of Extraordinary Gentleman* – and directed *Comic Book Villains*, which he also wrote.

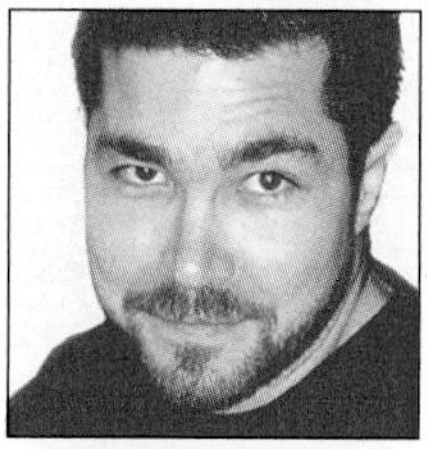

Hailed as "an instant legend" by writer Brian Michael Bendis, Italian artist **Gabriele Dell'Otto** established his reputation in the European comic-book industry with a series of painted covers for Panini. Dell'Otto's stunning work caught Marvel's attention, leading to a career-making assignment on the blockbuster *Secret War.* Propelled by Dell'Otto's stunning, fully painted work, the series became an instant sell-out and earned the artist *Wizard* magazine's prestigious "Breakout Talent of the Year" award in 2004.

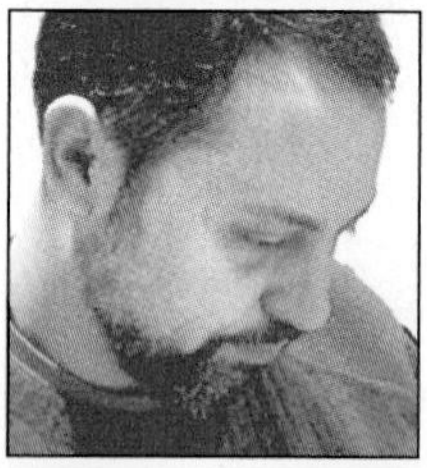

One of many Italian illustrators to find success in the United States in recent years, **Werther Dell'Edera** is quickly making his name as an artist capable of setting intense, simmering moods that can just as easily explode into unbelievable action. After drawing a run of the western comic *Loveless* at Vertigo, Dell'Edera came to Marvel, where he has worked with popular characters such as *Wolverine*, *Warpath* and *X-Force.*

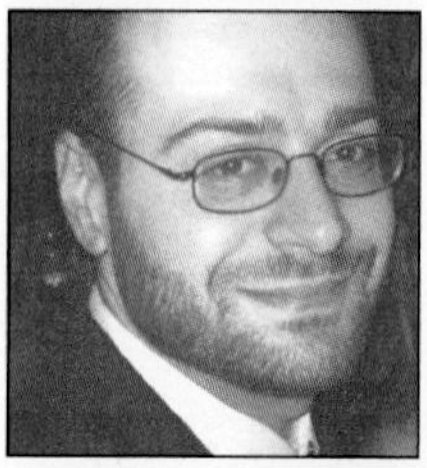

Joe Caramagna has been a regular writer and letterer for Marvel since 2007, most known for his work on *Iron Man and the Armor Wars*, *Marvel Universe: Ultimate Spider-Man*, *Amazing Spider-Man*, *Daredevil* and more. He has also written *Batman* and *Supergirl* shorts for DC Comics, and a series of *Amazing Spider-Man* novels for young readers.

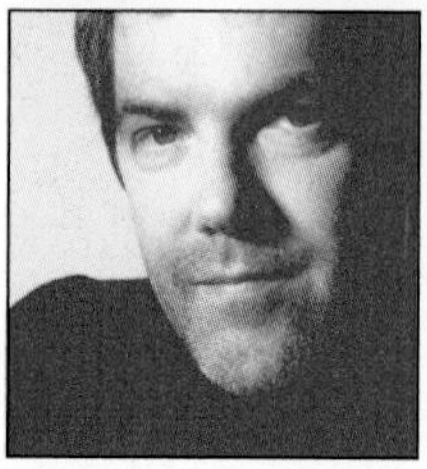

Designer and illustrator **Rian Hughes** began his career in the British music, advertising and fashion industries. His strips for *2000AD* and the short-lived *Revolver* with Grant Morrison and Mark Millar are collected in *Yesterday's Tomorrows* and *Tales from Beyond Science.* He has designed numerous logos, including *Batman and Robin*, *Batgirl* and *The Invisibles* for DC and *Iron Man*, *X-Men* and *Fantastic Four* for Marvel. Recent work includes writing and art for *Batman: Black and White.*

Behind the Scenes

Page 7

PAGE SEVEN

PANEL ONE: THE THUGS ARE IN THE TRUCK NOW--DRIVER'S PULLING ON THE GEARSHIFT, PASSENGER'S COUNTING CASH--BOTH REACTING TO A NOISE FROM UP.

DRIVER: C'mon. We got twelve more STOPS before--

SFX: t-TONK

PASSENGER: WHAT WAS THAT?

PANEL TWO, BIG: TO THEIR HORROR, SPIDER-MAN VAULTS ONTO THE HOOD OF THEIR TRUCK, LANDING IN A SQUATTING POSITION FACING THEM.

SPIDEY: What are you boys ON? DRYER SHEETS?

MEN/burst: AAAAAAAH!

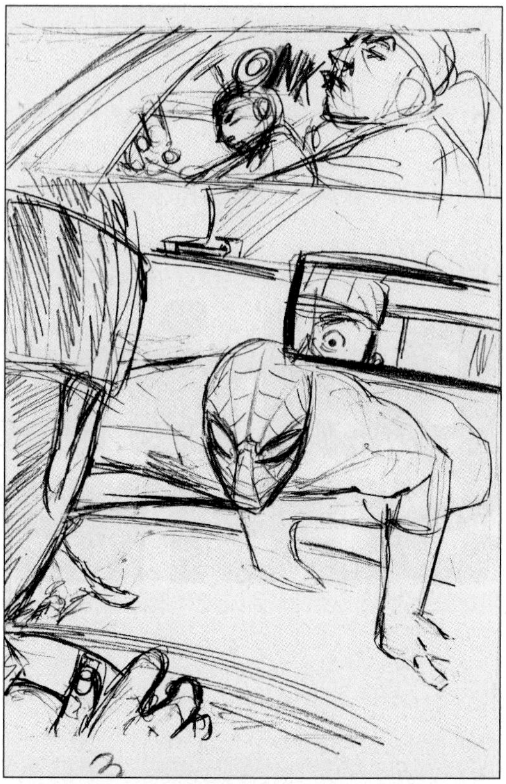

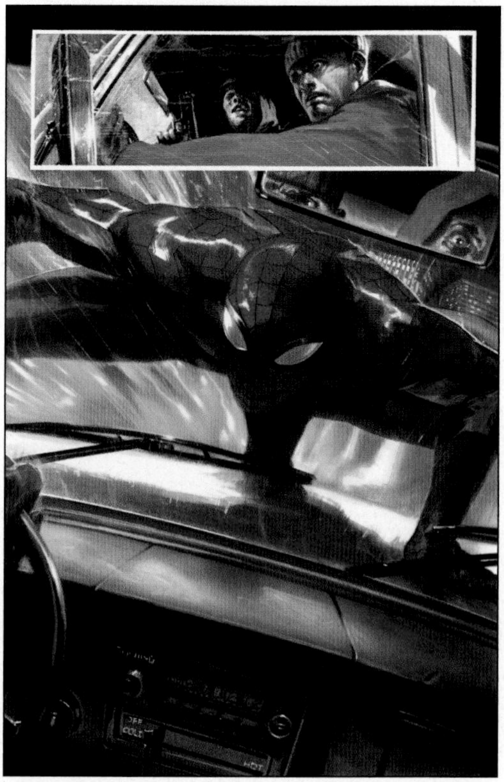

Script, layout, final art

Page 14

PAGE FOURTEEN

PANEL ONE/BIG: OUTSIDE. A SUPER-HIGH-TECH SILENT AIR TRANSPORT HOVERS IN THE AIR OUTSIDE PETE'S BUILDING, REELING PETE AND THE SOLDIERS TOWARDS IT!

PETER CAP: --maybe I should start taking this a little more SERIOUSLY.

PANEL TWO: TIGHT ON PETE'S HANDS BEHIND HIS BACK, SNAPPING THE ROPE.

SFX: whKSSH

Script, layout, final art

Page 17

PAGE SEVENTEEN

PANEL ONE: AS THE PURSUING AIRCRAFT OPENS FIRE ON THE FLEEING CONVERTIBLE, PETE GAPES/GETS HIS FIRST GOOD LOOK AT THE DRIVER-- A BEAUTIFUL BROWN-HAIRED WOMAN ABOUT HIS AGE.

PETE: Not unless there's a JET ENGINE under the hood of
             this thing!

PETE: You KNOW me?

DRIVER: I've seen pictures.

PETER: Who ARE you?

DRIVER: My name is TERESA PARKER.

PANEL TWO, BIG: FOCUS ON THE DRIVER AS THE CAR ROARS DOWN THE STREET TOWARDS US, THE PURSUING AIRCRAFT STRAFING THE STREET WITH GUNFIRE! IF WE SEE PETE IN THIS SHOT, HE'S GAPING AT HER IN SHOCK.

DRIVER: I'm your SISTER.

Script, layout, final art

Page 31

PAGE THIRTY-ONE

PANEL ONE: WE LOOK AT THE SCENE FROM CYCLONE'S P.O.V. WE SEE--

SPIDEY SWINGING IN, WITH A WEB ATTACHED TO THE CEILING. HE IS COMING STRAIGHT AT US, FEET ABOVE HEAD, YOU KNOW HE DOES HE IS FIRING WEB TOWARDS US.

THE CROWD AROUND HIM (BELOW HIM, IF WE'RE LOOKING AT SPIDEY AND HE'S IN THE AIR SWINGING AT US) ARE LOOKING UP AT HIM AGHAST. SOME ARE RUNNING FROM THE SCENE, SOME ARE FROZEN ON THE SPOT. MAYBE THE CROWD ARE CROPPED AT THE TORSO, BY OUR P.O.V. BEING DIRECTLY ON SPIDEY HIGHER ABOVE THEM.

SOME OF THE CROWD ARE LOOKING STRAIGHT AT US WITH TERROR (THEY'RE LOOKING AT CYCLONE AND NOT SPIDEY.)

LET'S GIVE THIS PANEL MORE THAN HALF THE PAGE. MORE LIKE TWO THIRDS OF THE PAGE, JUST TO SHOW SPIDEY AND THE CROWD AND THE CASINO DÉCOR AROUND THEM BEFORE IT ALL GETS BLOWN AROUND.

PETER CAPTION: Forget the GUNMEN.

PETER CAPTION: Now someone's sending COSTUMES after the Parkers!

SPIDEY: Hey, Cyclone, where are your manners?

SPIDEY: Your folks never teach you not to break wind in a crowded room?

PANEL TWO: CYCLONE AIMS A TIGHT WIND-VORTEX RIGHT AT SPIDEY.

CYCLONE/small: No one mentioned SPIDER-MAN...

CYCLONE: Stay OUT of this, wall-crawler...for YOUR sake!

Script, layout, final art

Page 45

PAGE FORTY-FIVE.
PANEL ONE.
EGYPT.
THIS IS A WIDE CINEMATIC SHOT OF EGYPT.
WE SEE THE CITY AS A SWEEPING PANORAMA. HAVE SOME "OLD CAIRO" IN IT TO MAKE IT VISUAL AND INTERNATIONAL BUT PUT IN A MODERN HOTEL IN THE MIDST OF IT (EVEN IF IT DOESN'T EXIST IN REALITY -- AT THE END OF THE DAY THIS IS A COMIC) SO THAT WE CAN TRACK IN PAST THE ORNATE/OLD TOWARDS THE MODERN HOTEL PENTHOUSE/ROOF PANEL BY PANEL.

CAPTION: Cairo.

MENTALLO: Can I go now?

PANEL TWO.
WE CLOSE IN ON THE HOTEL, BUT WE'RE STILL FAR ENOUGH OFF FROM IT, THAT THE PENTHOUSE ROOF/BALCONY (AND WHO'S ON IT, ISN'T TOO DISTINCT YET.)

MENTALLO: Mr. Fisk?

PANEL THREE.
WE NOW CLOSE IN TIGHTER ON THE HOTEL PENTHOUSE, SUCH THAT WE CAN NOW SEE MENTALLO AND FISK ON THE PENTHOUSE BALCONY/ROOF (BIG OPEN AREA -- LUXURIOUS), BUT THEY'RE STILL SMALL, SMALL IN SHOT FOR NOW.

FROM WHAT WE CAN SEE MENTALLO IS FURTHER BACK AWAY FROM THE BALCONY/ROOF RAILING WITH FISK CLOSE TO IT, LOOKING OUT AT THE CITY WITH HIS BACK TO MENTALLO.

MENTALLO: Mr. Fisk, I've done all you asked of me, and my head won't stop hurting, so I repeat...

PANEL FOUR.
WE'RE NOW IN THE AIR, FACING THE PENTHOUSE BALCONY/ROOF. FISK IS STANDING THERE TO ONE SIDE OF PANEL, FACING US, LOOKING OUT AT THE CITY.

MENTALLO IS TO THE OTHER SIDE OF PANEL, FURTHER FROM US, FACING US TOO AS HE LOOKS AT THE BACK OF FISK'S HEAD.

MENTALLO: ...May I please go?

KINGPIN: I have always prided myself on never punishing well-thought, honest question, Mr. Frumm.

PANEL FIVE.
SIDE-ON MED SHOT/PROFILE SHOT OF KINGPIN STILL LOOKING OFF PANEL AT THE CITY, STILL TREATING MENTALLO AS A MINOR INCONVENIENCE.

KINGPIN: That is not one.

PANEL SIX.
TIGHTER CU OF KINGPIN, FACING HIM AS HE LOOKS OUT AT THE CITY. HE'S BASICALLY LOOKING AT US IN THE FACE.

KINGPIN: Be thankful I still need your head attached to your SPINE.

Script, layout, final art

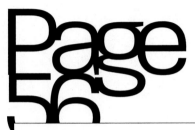

Page 56

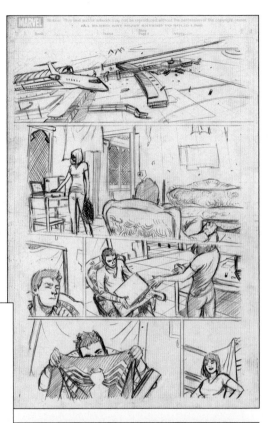

PAGE FIFTY-SIX.
PANEL ONE.
EGYPT. A SMALL AIRPORT RUNWAY. TERESA'S JET IN MIDGROUND,
PYRAMIDS IN BACKGROUND. ON THE RUNWAY, OFF THE PLANE, TERESA AND
PETER TAKE POSSESSION OF A WAITING JEEP FROM A SALUTING SOLDIER.
WHATEVER PETER'S WEARING, IT HAS LONG SLEEVES AND LONG PANTS.

PETER CAP: So the flight to Egypt is anything but boring.
Teresa has a million questions.

PETER CAP: But also a change of clothes.

PANEL TWO
TERESA: Thank you for losing the costume.

PETER: What was LEFT of it smelled like a barbecue gone
horribly wrong. Not much point in hanging on, but that leaves
Spidey OUT of the rest of this mission.

PANEL THREE.
TERESA/off: Not necessarily.

PANEL FOUR
TERESA: I had my people whip up a little something. They didn't
ask why or for who, I didn't say.

TERESA: We had to make do with materials at hand, and I guessed
at the size, but...

PANEL SIX.
AS THEY RIDE INTO THE DESERT, PETE HOLDS UP HIS BLACK SPIDER-MAN
COSTUME.

TERESA: ...you're back in black.

PETER: Cool.

Script, layout, final art

Page 80s

PAGE EIGHTY.
PANEL ONE.
KINGPIN, MERCS AND TERESA ARE ALL FELLED BY THE IMPACT OF THE
NEARBY CRASH!

PANEL TWO.
GROANING, HIS COSTUME TORN IN PLACES, A LITTLE BLOODY, SPIDEY
CRAWLS FROM THE WRECKAGE.

SPIDEY: =nnNNGGH--!=

PETER CAP: Looks like Cairo's another neighborhood SPIDER-MAN
gets to be friendly in.

PETER CAP: Hope they put that on my TOMBSTONE, because I'm
not sure I'm walking AWAY from this one.

SPIDEY/burst: TERESA! YOU OKAY? TERESA!

PANEL THREE.
BAM! SPIDEY'S SUCKER-PUNCHED FROM BEHIND BY KINGPIN!

SPIDEY/burst: =GNNNGH!=

Script, layout, final art

PAGE EIGHTY-ONE
PANELS.
HOWEVER YOU FEEL LIKE CHOREOGRAPHING IT--KINGPIN BEATS ON
WEAKENED SPIDEY UNTIL SPIDEY MANAGES TO KICK HIM INTO THE GIANT
HOLE IN THE GROUND LEFT BY THE SLEEPER. KINGPIN FALLS.

[Banter to come]

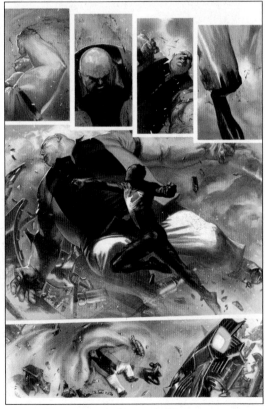

Script, layout, final art

Cover design

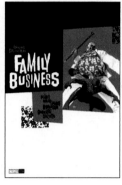

Some of Rian Hughes' alternative
cover design concepts

Also available

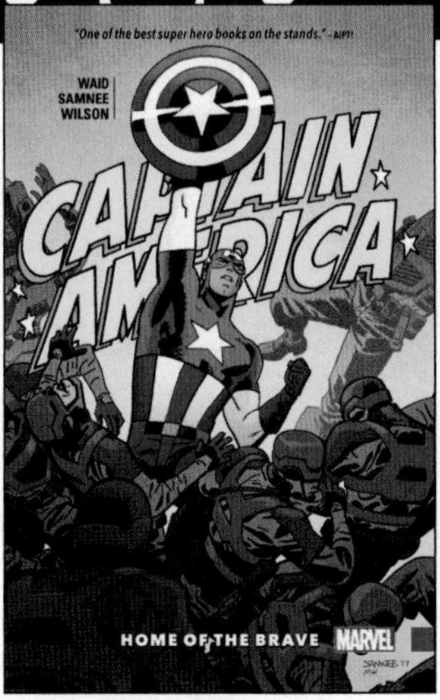
"One of the best super hero books on the stands."
WAID
SAMNEE
WILSON
CAPTAIN AMERICA
HOME OF THE BRAVE
MARVEL

CAPTAIN AMERICA BY WAID & SAMNEE: HOME OF THE BRAVE
978-1-302-90992-5

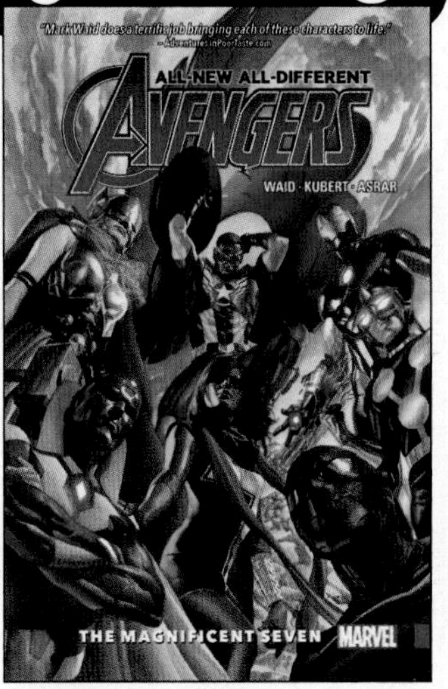
ALL-NEW ALL-DIFFERENT
AVENGERS
WAID · KUBERT · ASRAR
THE MAGNIFICENT SEVEN
MARVEL

ALL-NEW, ALL-DIFFERENT AVENGERS VOL. 1: THE MAGNIFICENT SEVEN
978-0-7851-9967-0

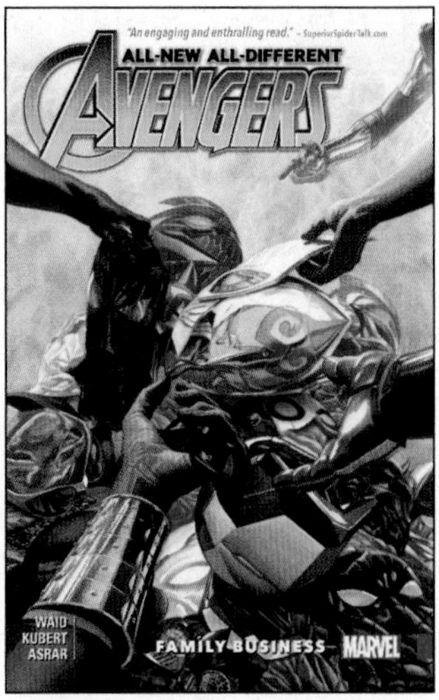
"An engaging and enthralling read."
ALL-NEW ALL-DIFFERENT
AVENGERS
WAID
KUBERT
ASRAR
FAMILY BUSINESS
MARVEL

ALL-NEW, ALL-DIFFERENT AVENGERS VOL. 2: FAMILY BUSINESS
978-0-7851-9968-7

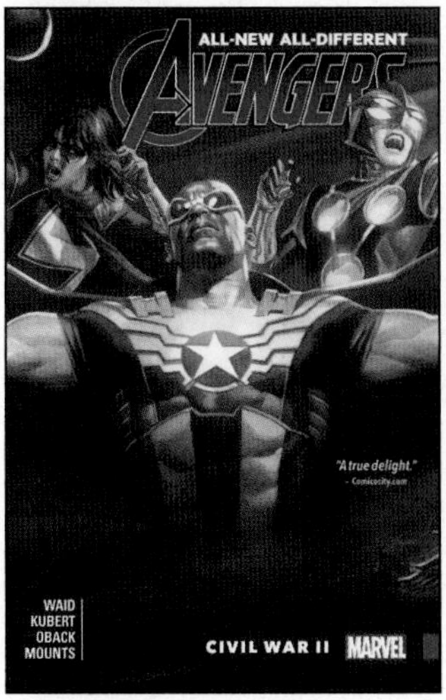
ALL-NEW ALL-DIFFERENT
AVENGERS
"A true delight."
WAID
KUBERT
OBACK
MOUNTS
CIVIL WAR II
MARVEL

ALL-NEW, ALL-DIFFERENT AVENGERS VOL. 3: CIVIL WAR II
978-1-302-90236-0

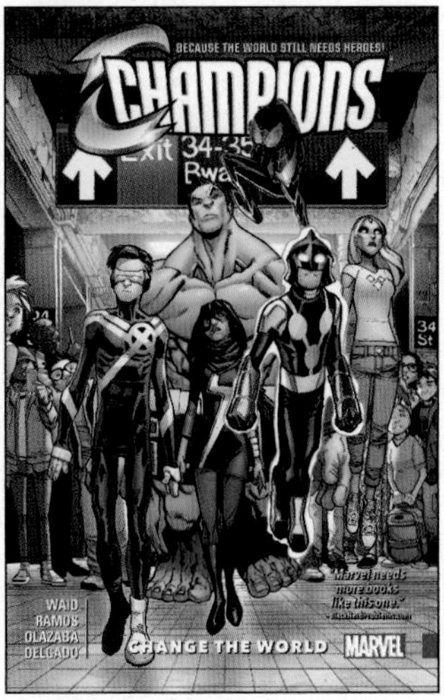
BECAUSE THE WORLD STILL NEEDS HEROES!
CHAMPIONS
WAID
RAMOS
OLAZABA
DELGADO
CHANGE THE WORLD
MARVEL

CHAMPIONS VOL. 1: CHANGE THE WORLD
978-1-302-90618-4

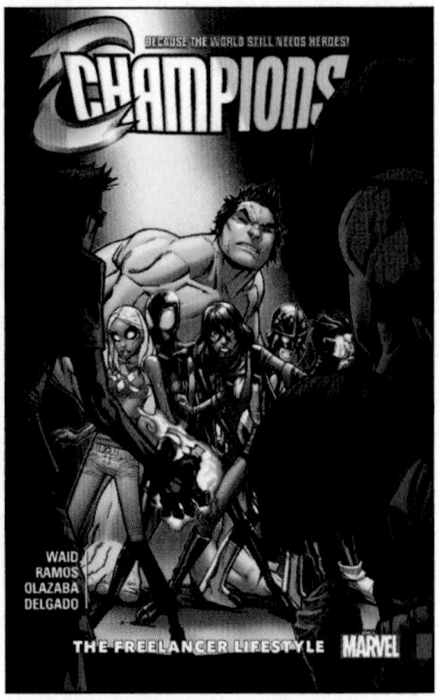
BECAUSE THE WORLD STILL NEEDS HEROES!
CHAMPIONS
WAID
RAMOS
OLAZABA
DELGADO
THE FREELANCER LIFESTYLE
MARVEL

CHAMPIONS VOL. 2: THE FREELANCER LIFESTYLE
978-1-302-90619-1

An abomination, long thought buried,
has resurfaced in a war-torn land.
But now it wears an American flag.
Faced with another nightmare reborn,
Captain America will not stand for yet more
death at the hands of a ghost from his
past. Haunted by his greatest shame, Thor
must renew the hunt for a familiar beast.
At their side, an assemblage of allies united
to end the threats no one of them could
face alone. They are soldiers. Warriors.
Comrades-in-arms. Mighty heroes led by a
living legend, stronger together than apart.
They are the Avengers.

Avengers: Endless Wartime

Warren Ellis, **Mike McKone** and **Jason Keith**
978-0-7851-8468-3

When Titan falls, Planet Ultron rises! It was another glorious victory for the Mighty Avengers. Good triumphed over evil and Ultron was shot into space, never to be seen again — or so they thought. Now, years later, the homicidal artificial intelligence — so long devoted to ending life on Earth — has found a new world to conquer...one with its own horrific legacy. To save his home planet of Titan, Thanos' brother Starfox must seek the aid of his former allies — but the Avengers he finds are radically different from the ones he once knew. Among them is Ultron's creator Giant-Man — and when Hank Pym confronts his now planet-sized "son," the responsibilities of fatherhood have never loomed so large. Rick Remender (*Uncanny Avengers*) and Jerome Opeña (*Avengers*) unleash Ultron's full robotic rage on Earth's Mightiest Heroes!

Avengers: Rage Of Ultron

RICK REMENDER
JEROME OPEÑA
PEPE LARRAZ
MARK MORALES
MARVEL OGN
AVENGERS
RAGE OF
ULTRON

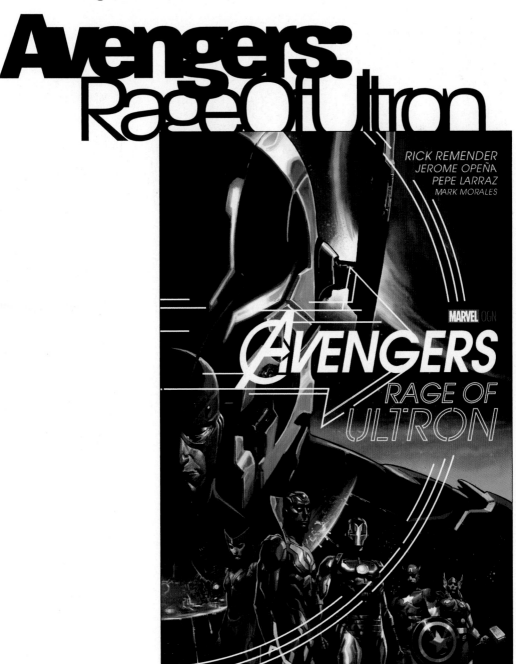

Rick Remender and **Jerome Opeña**
978-0-7851-9040-0